Mama Bell's
Big Family Cooking

100+ Big-Batch
Homestyle Recipes
*Your Family Is
Gonna Love!*

HEATHER BELL
of @justthebells10

Adams Media
New York   London   Toronto   Sydney   New Delhi

Adams Media
An Imprint of Simon & Schuster, LLC
100 Technology Center Drive
Stoughton, Massachusetts 02072

First Adams Media hardcover edition October 2024

ADAMS MEDIA and colophon are registered trademarks of Simon & Schuster, LLC.

Simon & Schuster: Celebrating 100 Years of Publishing in 2024

For information about special discounts for bulk purchases, please contact Simon & Schuster Special Sales at 1-866-506-1949 or business@simonandschuster.com.

The Simon & Schuster Speakers Bureau can bring authors to your live event. For more information or to book an event, contact the Simon & Schuster Speakers Bureau at 1-866-248-3049 or visit our website at www.simonspeakers.com.

Interior design by Colleen Cunningham and Erin Alexander
Interior images © 123RF/Aleksandra Novakovic, aarengoldin, Serhii Holdin
Interior photographs by Nathan Rega, Harper Point Photography unless otherwise noted
Food stylist: Kira Friedman
Chefs: Martine English, Christine Tarango, Kira Friedman

Manufactured in the United States of America

10 9 8 7 6 5 4 3 2 1

Library of Congress Cataloging-in-Publication Data
Names: Bell, Heather (Cookbook writer), author.
Title: Mama Bell's big family cooking / Heather Bell of @justthebells10.
Description: First Adams Media hardcover edition. | Stoughton, Massachusetts: Adams Media, 2024. | Includes index.
Identifiers: LCCN 2024015056 | ISBN 9781507222614 (hc) | ISBN 9781507222621 (ebook)
Subjects: LCSH: Cooking. | LCGFT: Cookbooks.
Classification: LCC TX714 .B3883 2024 | DDC 641.5--dc23/eng/20240410
LC record available at https://lccn.loc.gov/2024015056

ISBN 978-1-5072-2261-4
ISBN 978-1-5072-2262-1 (ebook)

Contents

CHAPTER 1. **One Dish Casserole Recipes** • 19

There was a city girl named Heather who moved to the country. She learned to make one dish meals that were simple and quick.

CHAPTER 2. **Grilling and Barbecue Recipes** • 45

She met a hardworking farm boy named Luke who was raised on a dairy farm and was a master at the grill.

CHAPTER 3. **Breakfast Recipes** • 67

They tried to have a family with no success and after four years adopted their first son David, whose favorite meal was breakfast.

CHAPTER 4. **Fun Pizza-Themed Recipes and Then Some** • 89

After becoming foster parents, they adopted Joshua. He overcame many obstacles in his life and learned to make meals with Mom, including pizzas.

CHAPTER 5. **Land and Sea Recipes** • 111

After the Bells tried for eight long years to have a baby, Gideon *was born. He loves to fish and spend time outdoors.*

CHAPTER 6. **Mexican-Inspired Favorites** • 135

*Three years later, the boys became big brothers to Izabella, "*Izzy,*" their new sister. She always pulled a stool beside Mom to help make dinner. Her favorite meal is tacos.*

CHAPTER 7. **Super-Easy Slow Cooker Meals** • 157

Hailey came into their lives. She'd prayed to have a big family, to live on a farm, and to go to church. She introduced Mom to making big meals in a slow cooker.

CHAPTER 8. **The Bell Family's Favorite Cookies** • 179

Three brothers came along, and the family knew immediately that they would complete the family. Robert is the "cookie monster" because of his love for all kinds of Mom's cookies.

CHAPTER 9. **Italian-Themed Recipes** • 201

The three boys were neighbors before they moved in, and Brendon *used to knock on the door every time Mom made spaghetti to ask to eat dinner with the family.*

CHAPTER 10. **Chili and Soup Recipes** • 227

Noah *is the youngest of the three brothers and completed the family perfectly. At first, he was quiet and always asked to eat soup—it didn't matter what kind.*

Preface

IF YOU WOULD HAVE asked me several years ago when I was cooking for our big family of ten if any of the many, *many* meals I have made would eventually be shared in a cookbook of my own, I would have laughed.

Why? Because I just assumed the big, filling, homestyle meals I make are the same as every family might make. But when our family started sharing our lives on social media, I noticed people were very interested in the ways we ran our farm, did chores, took care of the house, and especially what we ate. This was a little odd to me because I didn't feel like our family meals were any different from the rest of the world's meals. Sure, there are ten of us, and between my kids, their friends, and the workers on our farm, I often have to make meals big enough to feed a small army! But I was shocked that others were so interested in how I prepare meals and grocery shop on such a large scale and also how I store our food.

I have always loved cooking and baking for my loved ones, and each time our family grew on our adoption journey, I had to expand my recipes and create new ones that helped each child feel welcomed and comfortable. But it wasn't until we hopped on the social media train that I realized how interesting cooking for our unique big family was. And through our followers' excitement and anticipation over me sharing each recipe, I started to embrace cooking even more. It became a joy, and I began cooking not only for our family of ten but for hundreds, then thousands, and believe it or not, millions of people. Plus, our followers gave me the name Mama Bell, which has caught on so much that people now are shocked when I share that I have an actual name! But I don't mind "Mama Bell" because it has grown on me. So, I'm a "mama" to millions now.

Nowadays, I can't wait to grab my handy yellow notebook and create a new recipe to share with my family and followers. I soon realized that cooking was how I showed my family that I was thankful for all they do to make our family successful and how much I love each one of them. It was a wonderful journey I went through and now I have the amazing opportunity to share these recipes and our family's adoption journey with each one of you. Enjoy!

Introduction to
Mama Bell's Big Family Cooking

HI THERE, my name is Heather Bell, but people call me "Mama Bell." I am a mom to eight very active and always hungry children.

If you would have told me twenty-seven years ago that I would marry a farm boy raised on a dairy farm, own four thousand laying hens, raise Clydesdale horses, plus be a mother to eight children, I would have looked at you like you were crazy. You see, I set certain goals for myself, but it turns out God had other plans. It was 1994 and I was to graduate that spring and head off to medical school when I bumped into a strong and handsome boy, and just like that, my life was forever changed.

You may be thinking, "Wow, she must have grown up in the kitchen cooking next to her mother and learning all these wonderful recipes." Well, before I married my husband, Luke, believe it or not I had never even cooked an egg or boiled water, never mind made breakfast, lunch, or dinner. The kitchen was foreign to me, and I had no interest or desire in cooking anything for anyone. My husband, however, grew up on a dairy farm with a hardworking mother who cooked the majority of their meals from scratch, and the meals were big enough to feed an entire army. I knew right then I would have big shoes to fill if I was gonna even come close to making meals like hers.

Two important women in my life gave me the push I needed to start learning how to cook for my new husband. My mother-in-law, Dodie Bell, and my mom, Sheila Storey, loved cooking for their big families, and I could tell they enjoyed being in the kitchen because that was one of the many ways they showed how much they loved their families—through cooking. Now that I was a new wife, I was ready for these two important women in my life to guide me when it came to cooking for my new husband and my future family.

I was determined that the first meal I cooked for my husband would "knock his socks off." I had to find the perfect meal, but I was so nervous because I had absolutely no idea what I was doing. Finally, after hours of searching, I found it! This would be the test to see if I had the makings of a real cook. It was called Sour Cream and Chive Chicken, and it turned out amazing. Success! This first dinner gave me the encouragement I needed to embrace the kitchen more and become comfortable in creating meals all on my own. **Here is the recipe for the first meal I ever cooked so you can make it too:**

Sour Cream *and* Chive Chicken

This first dinner gave me the encouragement I needed to embrace the kitchen more and become comfortable in creating meals all on my own.

Prep Time: 30 minutes
Cook Time: 60 minutes
Yields: 8 servings

Ingredients:

4 cups Italian seasoned bread crumbs

1½ tablespoons salt, divided

1½ tablespoons ground black pepper, divided

1 tablespoon onion powder

1 tablespoon smoked paprika

2 cups salted butter, melted

1 (5-pound) whole chicken, innards removed, cut into pieces

8 medium sweet Vidalia onions, peeled and halved

1 (5-pound) bag yellow potatoes, peeled and cut into chunks

1 cup salted butter

1 cup all-purpose flour

4 cups chicken broth

2 cups heavy cream

1 (8-ounce) container sour cream

1 bunch fresh chives, chopped

Steps:

1. Preheat oven to 400°F.

2. In a medium shallow bowl or pie plate, combine bread crumbs with all the dry seasonings, except ½ tablespoon each of salt and pepper. Whisk and set aside.

3. Into a second medium shallow bowl or pie plate, pour in melted butter. Coat each piece of chicken in butter and then in bread crumb mixture.

4. Place coated chicken and onion halves throughout 2 greased 9" × 13" casserole dishes. Drizzle remaining melted butter over onions and sprinkle with leftover bread crumb mixture. Bake for 45 minutes.

5. While chicken is cooking, place potatoes into a large pot of boiling water for 20 minutes over medium heat. Once tender, drain and add 1 cup butter. Use a hand mixer to whip the mixture. Set aside.

6. Remove chicken from the oven and carefully pour drippings into a large saucepan. Add flour and remaining ½ tablespoon each of salt and pepper. Whisk over medium heat until a paste forms, about 2 minutes. Let simmer for 2 minutes, then slowly add broth while whisking. Next, add heavy cream and sour cream. Continue to whisk until cream thickens, about 5 minutes. Reduce heat to low and let simmer for 5 minutes, stirring often.

7. Serve chicken and onions with mashed potatoes topped with gravy. Sprinkle with fresh chives.

It's amazing to me how one meal could change how I looked at cooking for the next twenty-seven years. During my "awakening" in the kitchen, a lot started happening in the Bell family. Our journey to become parents definitely didn't go as we'd planned. After four long years of dealing with the heartache of infertility, we became parents to David Luke-Amos Bell through private adoption. Not only that, but within the following ten years we became foster parents and adopted six more children: Joshua, Izabella, Hailey, Robert, Brendon, and Noah. In the middle of this bustle of children coming in and out of our home, after eight long and trying years of dealing with infertility, we were surprised to find out that I was pregnant with my son Gideon.

While being foster parents, we never really knew when a child would come into our home or how long they would stay. Becoming a mother to eight children really challenged my cooking skills in preparing meals for so many different ages. I needed to make bigger portions that would go far, something we could heat up later just in case new children showed up, and meals that these new children would actually eat. I definitely made sure that I had Nana's Famous Chocolate Chip Cookies on hand at any given time to share with these sweet children coming into our home and also made sure not to forget to pour a glass of cold milk to dip the cookies into. When you're hurting, there is just something about a glass of milk and a cookie to take away the tears, even if just for that moment.

All of these wonderful experiences and opportunities have helped to prepare me to continue cooking big family meals for our family of ten, and everyone knows that the Bell family door is always open to anyone who might need a hot meal and a place to stay for as long as needed.

WELCOME

Sunday	Mama Bell's Famous Meatloaf
Monday	Tuna Noodle Casserole
Tuesday	Cast Iron Million Dollar Tater Tot Casserole
Wednesday	Grinder Sliders
Thursday	Izzy's Slow Cooker Taco Chili
Friday	Creamy Shrimp and Grits
Saturday	Cast Iron Cowboy Beans

MASON

I LOVE YOU LIKE BISCUITS AND GRAVY

MASON

There's No Such Thing As Too Much BUTTER

MASON

HEY good Lookin' WHATCHA GOT COOKIN'?

About My Book

THE TABLE OF CONTENTS for my book doesn't look like the typical list of meals and recipes that you'd find in a normal cookbook because this cookbook is so much more than our family recipes: It is also the story of the new beginnings and sweet bonds that became the journey of the Bell family. Our hope is that as you read through these wonderful recipes you will become part of our adoption journey and see how God brought each of us together. Each chapter shares recipes that are our family's favorites, ones that each family member has prepared themselves, or ones that they ask me to make over and over again. But there's also something a little more special within each chapter: You'll get to learn more about each of my children's adoption stories and our prayers being answered after eight years to have a child naturally. Cooking has been, and still is, a big part of our family because it brings us together every single day to share all that is going on in our lives.

Chapter 1 starts with me, Mama Bell, and my one dish casserole recipes. My husband has called me the "One Dish Wonder," and after thinking about it, I'd say he was right.

I like to create meals that have veggies, meats, cheeses, and something special in just one dish. So I guess you can say my meals are fast, simple, and *amazing*.

Chapter 2 is all about grilling and barbecue recipes and so it is dedicated to my husband, Luke, who is the best at showing his many cooking skills when it comes to grilling. It's not uncommon to look outside and see him cooking on both grills. He is my outdoors cooking guy; he is all about finding different spices to add extra flavor to make the best burgers, brisket, and veggies.

My oldest, David, was the first child we adopted and the one who made me a mom. He would eat breakfast for all three meals if he could. Chapter 3 is dedicated to him and his love of all things breakfast. His all-time favorite recipe is Homemade Buttermilk Biscuits and Gravy, so I make sure to put some aside each time I make it so he can have leftovers for the next meal. Every time I make a special breakfast, he smells it from upstairs and will be the first one in the kitchen holding a fork with a big smile on his face.

My sweet Joshua came into our home when he was two years old, and just like that,

David became a big brother. Joshua loved cooking with me, and when I asked him what he would like to make, his answer was always homemade pizzas. Over the years he has created some really cool pizza-themed meals for dinner, and Chapter 4 is great for him and other kids who love fun pizza recipes.

Gideon was born after eight long years of praying. When he was little, I could never get him to come inside; he would play in the puddles and explore the woods. That's why Chapter 5, which is our land and sea recipes, is perfect for him. When Gideon was younger, he would make fishing poles out of string and sticks and act like he caught fish for me to cook for dinner. Now that he's older he still enjoys making dinner for our family with all the fish he actually catches.

A few years later, the boys became big brothers to little Izzy. She has been my helper in the kitchen for as long as I can remember. Actually, I can't even remember a time when she didn't love helping me cook meals for our big family. She would hear me open the fridge, and I could hear little feet running in and her grabbing a stool to help me make dinner. Chapter 6 is Izzy's Mexican-themed meals for her love of this type of cuisine. Let me tell you, my daughter hands down makes the best homemade carnitas in the Upper Peninsula.

Three years later we adopted the cutest nine-year-old girl named Hailey. Izzy was so excited to have a big sister to hang out with, and they were inseparable. Hailey prayed to live on a farm, have a big family, and go to church. She really wasn't too interested in cooking until she was introduced to a slow cooker. Chapter 7 is super-easy slow cooker meals for Hailey. She was the one who introduced me to slow cooking; I actually never cooked with one until Hailey started making our big family dinners using it. I quickly realized how convenient it was to just dump and go a dinner—it's a real game changer.

Robert and his two little brothers came into our home shortly after Hailey. My mother would come visit and bring these beautiful, huge chocolate chip cookies, and Robert would eat pretty much every one, then ask her to make more. After several years my mother finally shared the recipe with me so I could make them for him whenever he asked. That's why Chapter 8, which is all about our family's favorite cookie recipes, is dedicated to Robert, my personal "cookie monster." Each one of us has a favorite cookie that I bake throughout the year. I took these basic recipes and built on them to create new recipes for Robert to try out. So far, I haven't baked a single cookie that Robert hasn't loved.

Brendon is the middle brother of the three, and when he moved in, he brought more happiness and laughter to our family. Chapter 9 is Italian-themed recipes, which Brendon asks me to cook every week, but his all-time favorite is my Homemade Spaghetti and Meatballs. Whenever I ask for dinner ideas, his response is always lasagna, meatballs, tortellini, or another Italian dinner idea. He loves to help in the kitchen, and he can make a seriously delicious manicotti. Whenever he's in the kitchen with me, not only do we laugh so much, but we also end up busting some moves.

Chapter 10 is chili and soup recipes and is the perfect end to our cookbook because Noah—our soup lover—was the one to complete our family. He is my quiet child with the biggest heart and used to come into the kitchen, put his chin on his hands, and just watch me cook. He loved being by me but never asked to help cook until fall because he is the chili-making master. His favorite thing was to take a piece of bread slathered with real butter and dip it into the chili or soup. He would take a bite of the bread right in the middle and would look up with a smile on his face and butter on each side of the great big smile. I'm kinda thinking he ate more bread than actual soup itself.

So now you see how our "not so typical" table of contents shares how our "not so typical" family came together. God knew that all ten of us needed each other to heal, find support, and build a family through love. This is why cooking has become my language of love—my way to show love to my family through the meals I make. I hope that our family story and *Mama Bell's Big Family Cooking* is a blessing to your family.

CHAPTER 1

One Dish Casserole Recipes

~✻~

There was a city girl named Heather *who moved to the country. She learned to make one dish meals that were simple and quick.*

I came to the realization that cooking is my language of love as I became a new wife and, before I knew it, a mother to eight very busy children. Throughout this amazing journey, cooking has been a huge part of our family because it is the one thing that brings us together every single day. When our big family sits down at the table, it's not only about eating a meal together but reconnecting as a family—sharing our day with each other, our disappointments, and our accomplishments. It gives us a chance to talk through these things together as a whole family and to help one another through love and encouragement. It's our time with no interruptions from the world. Just. Us. Ten. So, let's start at the beginning with my story.

I never thought that one day I would become a farm girl wearing Muck boots and walking through mud and manure every day. That was, until I met my future husband, Luke, who was raised on a dairy farm with his three siblings. Unlike my husband, my father was a sergeant in the air force, so our family traveled often from state to state. I grew up in a big family of ten, so I was familiar with how big families work—especially during mealtimes. My mother did a great job at making family meals that could feed her big crew, and the one thing I can vividly remember growing up was my house always smelling like freshly baked cookies. It didn't have to be a special occasion for my mother to whip up her cookies (Nana's Famous Chocolate Chip Cookies in Chapter 8) for us eight kids. I would come home every day from school and my mother would be playing the piano, and there on the dining room table sat a big plate of cookies, glasses, and milk waiting for us. Honestly, I never really thought much about how my mother prepared dinner and that she was constantly in the kitchen cooking, until I got married and started to have my own big family. Looking back, I realize that I have stepped into the very same position my mother was in when I was a young girl. Now that I am older, I appreciate all my mother did to provide us with big family meals that were simple and delicious.

My journey in becoming a mother wasn't the "typical" motherhood. My goal as a mother wasn't to have eight children or to be a mother figure to many other children who came in and out of our home during the thirteen years of being a foster parent. My plan was to get married at thirty-five years old and have twin girls, a perfect family of four. But God had other plans.

When I was diagnosed with infertility at twenty-one years old, I started to realize that "my plan" might not go quite as I expected. And then through fostering and adoption, our forever family grew very fast, and I had to learn how to cook big, like really big—like really, really *big*—meals. I had many mouths to feed with the children we adopted and other foster children who came in and out of our home weekly. I had to create meals that could feed a lot of little mouths that were kid and budget friendly.

Through the guidance of my mother, I learned how to plant a huge garden, harvest the veggies, and store them for future meals. My mother baked the best cookies, and she could throw down a dinner in no time and have it ready for my father when he came home from work. I wish I knew then how important it was to help my mother in the kitchen and watch how making dinner works. Oh boy! If only I had known that I too would become a mom to eight children.

Throughout the years I have mastered different recipes and by accident created new ones. Like other mothers, I have my favorite meals and ones that I avoid making. This might come as a surprise, but on some days I can be a lazy cook—that's why I prefer one dish casseroles. My husband calls me the "One Dish Wonder." I feel like casseroles are similar to dump and go desserts. You would be surprised how many different veggies you can hide in a good casserole (wink! wink!).

My kitchen is my happy place. Over the years, I have come to realize that cooking and baking are my language of love for the people I love most in the whole wide world. I'm so excited to share with you my favorite meals that started my journey with creating meals big enough for our family of ten—in just one dish. 🌹

Cast Iron Green Bean *and* Beef Casserole

Ingredients:
- 3 pounds 90/10 lean ground beef
- 1 tablespoon liquid aminos (or soy sauce)
- 1 tablespoon coconut oil
- 2 tablespoons minced fresh garlic
- 1 tablespoon dried thyme
- 1 tablespoon dried basil
- ½ tablespoon garlic salt
- 2 tablespoons dried minced onion
- 2 cups uncooked instant white rice
- 4 cups fresh green beans, ends trimmed
- 2 cups water

Steps:

1. Combine ground beef, liquid aminos, oil, minced garlic, thyme, basil, garlic salt, and minced onion in a 17" round cast iron pan over medium-high heat. Use a wooden spoon to break up the ground beef. Cook for 15 minutes, stirring often, or until beef is no longer pink.

2. Add rice, green beans, and water to the meat mixture and stir to combine.

3. Reduce heat to low and simmer for 15 minutes or until rice is tender. Fluff with a fork and then serve.

This was the first meal that I made using my huge cast iron pan. I was intimidated by cast iron for years because I thought it was only for campfire cooking. This meal came about because we were low on food one day and I needed a meal that was fast and inexpensive. I had forgotten to take anything out for dinner and I got home late—a bad combination! I literally started grabbing food ingredients and different spices and mixed away. To my surprise it turned out great and my family loved it.

Prep Time: 20 minutes
Cook Time: 30 minutes
Yields: 12 servings

Sloppy Joe Corn Bread Casserole

Sloppy joes were a go-to meal for me when my children were little because they were easy to make, and I could make quite a bit knowing there would be leftovers. We ate it so often that I wanted to create a dish that would have the same concept, but that I could turn into an all-in-one casserole meal. I added some veggies and paired it with corn bread, and it was a win for our family. This is a dish that even the little ones will eat.

Prep Time: 20 minutes
Cook Time: 1 hour
Yields: 10 servings

Filling Ingredients:

2 pounds 90/10 lean ground beef

2 pounds ground Italian sausage

2 tablespoons hot sauce

1/4 cup yellow mustard

1/4 cup ketchup

1 1/2 cups barbecue sauce, divided

2 tablespoons minced fresh garlic

2 tablespoons garlic salt

3 tablespoons dried minced onion

Corn Bread Ingredients:

2 cups corn bread mix

1 large egg

1 1/2 cups whole milk

3 tablespoons bacon grease (or shortening)

1 (4-ounce) can diced green chilies

2 cups shredded medium Cheddar cheese

Steps:

1. Preheat oven to 375°F.

2. **Make the Filling:** In a large skillet, combine Filling ingredients except 1/2 cup barbecue sauce and mix together. Cook over medium-high heat for 15 minutes, stirring occasionally.

3. Add remaining 1/2 cup barbecue sauce to meat mixture and continue cooking until meat is fully cooked, about 7–10 minutes. Set Filling aside and start Corn Bread.

4. **Make the Corn Bread:** In a large bowl, combine corn bread mix, egg, milk, bacon grease, and chilies. Stir well.

5. Pour meat filling into a greased 10" × 15" casserole dish and spread out evenly. Top with an even layer of cheese and then a layer of Corn Bread mixture, making sure to smooth out evenly.

6. Bake for 40 minutes. Serve.

Big Mac Tater Tot Casserole

Tater Tot casserole is a lot of fun to make. When I told my children that I was making this, they hovered over me the entire time until it was ready to eat. Our entire family was anxious to see if this would taste just like the famous Big Mac burger. Honestly, it tasted exactly like it and was soooo good. There are so many ingredients you can add to a Tater Tot casserole to make it your own and change up the flavors. I make sure to have many 10-pound bags of Tater Tots in the freezer just in case!

Prep Time: 30 minutes
Cook Time: 55 minutes
Yields: 12 servings

Ingredients:

2 pounds 90/10 lean ground beef

1 large yellow onion, peeled and diced

1 tablespoon ground yellow mustard

1 tablespoon onion powder

1 tablespoon dried minced onion

1 tablespoon minced fresh garlic

1 (16-ounce) bottle Thousand Island dressing, divided

1 (10-ounce) jar chunky dill relish

2 cups shredded medium Cheddar cheese

1 (2-pound) bag frozen Tater Tots

1 cup shredded iceberg lettuce

1 tablespoon sesame seeds

Steps:

1. Preheat oven to 375°F.

2. Combine beef, diced onion, dry seasonings, and garlic in a 10-quart stockpot and cook over medium heat for 15 minutes or until meat is cooked through, stirring occasionally. Remove from heat.

3. Add in dressing (reserving ¼ cup) and relish. Mix together and then pour into a greased 10" × 15" casserole dish.

4. Layer cheese on top of meat mixture and then top with Tater Tots.

5. Bake for 40 minutes. Remove from oven and let stand for 15 minutes.

6. Drizzle on remaining ¼ cup dressing, then top with lettuce and sesame seeds. Serve.

Cast Iron Chicken Potpie

Chicken potpie is my son Robert and daughter Hailey's favorite meal of all time. I have made this dish so many times that I could easily make it in my sleep! What's great about Cast Iron Chicken Potpie is that you can make a homemade crust or use a premade store-bought one, and it will still turn out great. Brushing the top crust with egg white makes it flaky and delicious. You can also brush the top with melted butter and sprinkle with dried parsley.

Prep Time: 30 minutes
Cook Time: 1 hour and **20** minutes
Yields: 12–14 servings

Homemade Chicken Broth Ingredients:

3 pounds boneless, skinless chicken breasts

8 cups water

4 tablespoons dried Italian seasoning

2 tablespoons dried minced onion

2 tablespoons dried parsley

2 tablespoons minced fresh garlic

Veggie Filling Ingredients:

1 cup salted butter

1 large yellow onion, peeled and diced

4 cups chopped celery

4 cups peeled and chopped carrots

1 (12-ounce) bag frozen peas

Roux Ingredients:

$\frac{1}{2}$ cup salted butter

$\frac{1}{2}$ tablespoon salt

$\frac{1}{2}$ tablespoon ground black pepper

1 tablespoon minced fresh garlic

1 tablespoon dried parsley

1 tablespoon ground yellow mustard

1 cup all-purpose flour

8 cups Homemade Chicken Broth (from this recipe)

2 cups heavy cream

Additional Ingredients:

4 premade store-bought pie crusts, at room temperature

4 large egg whites, lightly beaten

Steps:

1. Preheat oven to 375°F.

2. **Make the Homemade Chicken Broth:** Combine all ingredients in an 8-quart saucepot. Cook over medium heat for 30 minutes or until the liquid has a deep yellow color. Transfer chicken to a large bowl and shred with a hand mixer. Set broth aside.

3. **Make the Veggie Filling:** Melt 1 cup butter in a large saucepan over medium heat. Add onion, celery, carrots, and peas to pan and sauté for 15 minutes or until veggies are tender, stirring occasionally. Set aside.

continued

continued

4. **Make the Roux:** In another large saucepan, melt ½ cup butter over medium heat, then add salt, pepper, garlic, parsley, mustard, and flour. Whisk continually until mixture forms a paste, about 2 minutes, and then let it simmer for 1 minute.

5. Slowly, add Homemade Chicken Broth to Roux paste while continually whisking over medium heat until the mixture thickens, about 3 minutes. Whisk in cream. Set aside.

6. Stack two pie crusts and roll them out together so they are a little bigger than the bottom of a 17" round cast iron pan. Place the rolled crust in the bottom of the 17" round cast iron pan. Then stack and roll out the other two crusts and set aside.

7. In a large bowl, combine shredded chicken, Veggie Filling, and Roux. Pour mixture onto the crust in the cast iron pan and then top with the other crust. Seal edges of crust together using a fork.

8. Using a butter knife, cut 12 (1") air holes into top crust and then brush entire crust with egg whites. Bake for 30 minutes. Serve.

Cast Iron Bunkhouse Stroganoff Pie

I grew up in the South, and my mother made beef Stroganoff often. I loved the creamy texture and flavor. I feel like this dish is a cross between a traditional beef Stroganoff recipe and a shepherd's pie. I bet topping it with a brown gravy would be great. You could also roll out 6" circles of crust and place this filling into the center, then fold over to make mini bunkhouse pasty pies. Pasties up north are served with brown gravy or ketchup.

Prep Time: 30 minutes
Cook Time: 1 hour and **10** minutes
Yields: 10–12 servings

Filling Ingredients:

4 pounds 90/10 lean ground beef

2 tablespoons Worcestershire sauce

1 tablespoon minced fresh garlic

1 tablespoon dried thyme

2 tablespoons dried minced onion

1 tablespoon salt

1 tablespoon ground black pepper

3 tablespoons dried parsley

1 large yellow onion, peeled and chopped

4 cups shredded carrots

2 cups beef broth

2 (8-ounce) blocks cream cheese

1 cup heavy cream

1 (22.6-ounce) can condensed cream of mushroom soup

1 cup bread crumbs

Crust Ingredients:

6 cups all-purpose flour

1 teaspoon ground black pepper

2 teaspoons salt

2 teaspoons white sugar

1 cup shortening

1 cup salted butter

4 large eggs, divided

1 cup plus 2 tablespoons whole milk, divided

Steps:

1. Preheat oven to 375°F.

2. **Make the Filling:** In a large saucepan, combine beef, Worcestershire sauce, garlic, dry seasonings, veggies, and broth. Cook over medium-high heat for 20 minutes or until meat is fully cooked and veggies are tender, stirring occasionally.

3. To this Filling, add cream cheese, heavy cream, and soup. Reduce heat to low and cook until cheese is melted with a smooth consistency, about 10 minutes, stirring occasionally.

4. Stir in bread crumbs and remove from heat.

continued

5. **Make the Crust:** In a large bowl whisk dry ingredients together, then cut in shortening and butter using a pastry cutter, fork, or food processor. Add 2 eggs and 1 cup milk and continue cutting into flour mixture until combined.

6. Knead dough until a ball forms. Divide into two equal parts. On a floured surface, roll each piece big enough to cover a 17" round cast iron pan. Set one Crust aside.

7. Cover bottom of pan with one of the Crusts. Pour Filling over the bottom Crust. Place the other Crust over Filling and seal edges together with a fork.

8. Using a butter knife, cut 12 (1") air holes in the top Crust.

9. In a small bowl, add remaining 2 eggs and remaining 2 tablespoons milk, whisk together, and then brush on top of the Crust.

10. Bake for 40 minutes. Serve.

Cast Iron Chicken *and* Spinach *with* Buttermilk Biscuits

This recipe is very nostalgic for me because it reminds me of the southern old-fashioned meals my mom made me when I was growing up. She would make fluffy biscuits quite a bit and pair them with homemade fried chicken and chicken potpie. This buttermilk biscuit recipe is so easy to make, and the biscuits come out light and fluffy—perfect with lots of butter and honey.

Prep Time: 30 minutes
Cook Time: 50 minutes
Yields: 10–12 servings

Filling Ingredients:
4 pounds boneless, skinless chicken breasts
1 cup salted butter, softened
1 large yellow onion, peeled and chopped
2 (10-ounce) bags frozen spinach, thawed and drained
2 tablespoons minced fresh garlic
2 tablespoons Dijon mustard
1 tablespoon garlic salt
1 tablespoon ground white pepper
1 teaspoon ground nutmeg
2 (2-ounce) jars chopped pimientos
2 large eggs, slightly beaten
2 cups sour cream

Biscuit Ingredients:
3 1/3 cups all-purpose flour
4 teaspoons baking powder
2 teaspoons salt
1 tablespoon dried parsley
1 tablespoon garlic powder
1 1/4 cups buttermilk
1 cup unsalted butter, softened

Steps:

1. Preheat oven to 375°F.

2. **Make the Filling:** To a large saucepan, add chicken, salted butter, and onion. Cook over medium heat for 20 minutes or until chicken is completely cooked, stirring occasionally.

3. Remove mixture from pan, place in a large bowl, and shred chicken with a hand mixer. Add spinach, garlic, mustard, all dry seasonings, pimientos, eggs, and sour cream. Stir well.

4. Pour Filling into a 17" round cast iron pan. Set aside.

5. **Make the Biscuits:** In a separate large bowl, combine all Biscuit ingredients and mix with a spoon. Using a scoop or serving tablespoon, drop dough onto Filling, making sure to cover the Filling evenly.

6. Bake for 30 minutes. Serve.

Mama Bell's Famous Meatloaf

If I had to pick my all-time favorite dish to make, it would be meatloaf because you can add so many different ingredients to it and create a totally new meatloaf recipe. It is so easy to make, and I love trying out different variations for my family. I have made everything from a 10-pound meatloaf to mini meatloaves, always serving them with mashed potatoes loaded with butter, salt, and pepper. My family also loves burgers, and so I recently made meatloaf burgers, and they turned out so good.

Prep Time: 20 minutes
Cook Time: 40 minutes
Yields: 10–12 servings

Ingredients:

2 pounds 90/10 lean ground beef

2 pounds ground Italian sausage

2 large yellow onions, peeled and chopped

1 tablespoon salt

1 tablespoon ground black pepper

$1/2$ teaspoon crushed red pepper flakes

2 teaspoons smoked paprika

2 tablespoons dried minced onion

2 tablespoons minced fresh garlic

4 large eggs

$1/2$ cup quick-cooking oats

2 tablespoons Dijon mustard

$1/4$ cup Worcestershire sauce

2 cups shredded Parmesan cheese

$1 1/2$ cups ketchup, divided

$1/2$ cup balsamic vinegar

2 teaspoons hot sauce

Steps:

1. Preheat oven to 400°F.

2. In a large bowl, combine all ingredients, reserving 1 cup ketchup, vinegar, and hot sauce for topping. Mix well and set aside.

3. In a medium bowl, combine reserved 1 cup ketchup, vinegar, and hot sauce. Mix well and set aside.

4. Pour meat mixture into a 17" round cast iron pan. Spread out evenly and brush topping mixture over meat.

5. Bake for 40 minutes or until meat is thoroughly cooked. Serve.

Tuna Noodle Casserole

This casserole is my husband's favorite meal of all time. When summertime hits, he constantly asks me to make him a cold tuna salad. So, I whip up a big batch and put it into containers for him to take to work every day. When the weather gets colder, he asks for this Tuna Noodle Casserole, which I make a double batch of because I know it will go fast in our house. Before my children eat, I make sure to put some aside for Luke's lunch the next day. Also, it stores well in the fridge and is just as tasty the next day.

Prep Time: 20 minutes
Cook Time: 40 minutes
Yields: 10–12 servings

Ingredients:

4 cups frozen mixed vegetables

1 (22.6-ounce) can condensed cream of mushroom soup

1 cup heavy cream

2 (12-ounce) cans tuna fish

2 (12-ounce) bags medium egg noodles, cooked according to package directions

2 tablespoons minced fresh garlic

1 tablespoon garlic salt

1 tablespoon ground black pepper

2 tablespoons dried minced onion

2 tablespoons dried parsley

4 cups shredded medium Cheddar cheese, divided

1/2 cup salted butter, softened

2 cups crushed butter crackers

Steps:

1. Preheat oven to 375°F.

2. In a large bowl, combine mixed veggies, soup, cream, tuna, noodles, minced garlic, garlic salt, pepper, minced onion, parsley, and 2 cups cheese and mix together.

3. Pour tuna mixture into 2 greased 9" × 13" casserole dishes, making sure to spread it out evenly.

4. Sprinkle each dish with 1 cup cheese and set aside.

5. In a small bowl, combine butter and crackers and stir together with a fork. Sprinkle on top of cheese layer.

6. Bake for 40 minutes. Serve.

Chicken Veggie-All Casserole

My husband's Grandma Lenhart made this as a side dish for Thanksgiving, and I couldn't get enough of it. I asked her for the recipe and started making it every Thanksgiving for our family. Her recipe had the veggies from a can, so I substituted fresh veggies instead and sautéed them in butter and garlic. I took it to another level by adding chopped chicken breast and more seasonings to create an entire casserole as the main dish. It still has that Grandma Lenhart feel but with Mama Bell's extras.

Prep Time: 20 minutes
Cook Time: 1 hour and **15** minutes
Yields: 12–14 servings

Ingredients:

2 cups peeled and chopped carrots

2 cups peeled and diced russet potatoes

1 cup chopped celery

2 large yellow onions, peeled and chopped

2 tablespoons minced fresh garlic

1 cup plus 4 tablespoons salted butter, divided

4 pounds boneless, skinless chicken breasts, cut into $1/2$" cubes

2 tablespoons dried parsley

2 tablespoons garlic salt

2 tablespoons garlic powder

2 cups mayonnaise

4 cups shredded medium Cheddar cheese, divided

2 (15-ounce) cans peas, drained

2 (15-ounce) cans lima beans, drained

2 (15.25-ounce) cans corn, drained

2 (14.5-ounce) cans green beans, drained

2 (8-ounce) cans whole water chestnuts, drained and chopped

4 cups crushed plain potato chips

Steps:

1. In a large saucepan, combine fresh veggies, minced garlic, and 4 tablespoons butter over medium heat. Cook until veggies are tender, about 15 minutes, stirring occasionally. Set aside.

2. In a separate large saucepan over medium heat, combine chicken, $1/2$ cup butter, parsley, garlic salt, and garlic powder and sauté until chicken is fully cooked, about 15 minutes, stirring occasionally. Set aside.

3. Preheat oven to 375°F.

4. In a large bowl, combine mayo, 2 cups cheese, peas, lima beans, corn, green beans, and water chestnuts. Mix with a spoon. Add the cooked veggies and chicken to the large bowl. Mix together and pour into a greased 10" × 15" casserole dish and spread out evenly. Top with remaining 2 cups cheese.

5. Melt remaining $1/2$ cup butter in a large glass bowl for 45 seconds in microwave and add potato chips. Using a fork, mix together. Sprinkle potato chip mixture over filling and cheese. Bake for 45 minutes. Serve.

Chicken Cordon Bleu Casserole

My favorite thing about chicken cordon bleu is the Swiss cheese and ham covered in creamy cheese sauce. I wanted to challenge myself to create a casserole-style dish that would be faster to make but still taste the same as the original. I added potatoes to make this comfort meal more filling to satisfy my seven hardworking guys.

Prep Time: 30 minutes
Cook Time: 1 hour and **10** minutes
Yields: 10 servings

Ingredients:

4 pounds boneless, skinless chicken breast tenderloins

1 cup salted butter, divided

2 tablespoons minced fresh garlic

1 tablespoon dried parsley

1 large yellow onion, peeled and diced

2 cups peeled and diced carrots

10 medium yellow potatoes, sliced thin

1 cup all-purpose flour

1 tablespoon salt

1 tablespoon ground black pepper

2 tablespoons dried minced onion

4 cups chicken broth

2 cups heavy cream

1 cup shredded Parmesan cheese

1 (8-ounce) package sliced Swiss cheese

1 (8-ounce) package sliced provolone cheese

1 (16-ounce) package sliced black forest ham

2 cups bread crumbs

1 tablespoon ground yellow mustard

1 tablespoon garlic salt

Steps:

1. Preheat oven to 375°F.

2. In a large saucepan, add chicken, ½ cup butter, 2 tablespoons minced garlic, and parsley. Cook over medium heat for 15 minutes or until chicken is fully cooked, stirring occasionally.

3. Add diced onions and carrots and continue cooking until veggies are tender, about 15 minutes, stirring occasionally.

4. Remove chicken mixture from pan, reserving drippings. Transfer mixture into the bottom of a greased 10" × 15" casserole dish.

5. Top chicken mixture with a layer of potato slices.

6. Add remaining ½ cup butter to drippings in saucepan and cook over low heat until butter is completely melted.

continued

continued

7. Add flour, salt, pepper, and minced onion. Whisk until a paste forms, about 2 minutes, and let simmer for 2 minutes.

8. Slowly add broth while continuing to whisk. Add cream and Parmesan and simmer for an additional 5 minutes while whisking, until thickened.

9. Pour a thin layer of roux over potatoes, about 3 cups.

10. Top with a layer of Swiss cheese, then provolone cheese, and lastly ham slices.

11. Pour remainder of roux over all ingredients.

12. In a small bowl, combine bread crumbs, mustard, and garlic salt and whisk together. Sprinkle on top of casserole.

13. Bake for 30 minutes. Serve.

Cast Iron Million Dollar Tater Tot Casserole

If you have a bunch of picky kids in your home, they are going to love this version of Tater Tot casserole. When I made this for the very first time, my children fought over who would get the last helping. The cream cheese makes this dish extra yummy. It's no wonder that it's become my fallback meal when I'm out of ideas for dinner. It helps that I am a cream cheese fan and am constantly looking for recipes to add it to. I always have at least a dozen blocks of cream cheese in my fridge!

Prep Time: 20 minutes
Cook Time: 1 hour and **25** minutes
Yields: 10–12 servings

Ingredients:

4 pounds 90/10 lean ground beef

2 tablespoons ground white pepper

1 tablespoon garlic salt

4 tablespoons dried minced onion

4 tablespoons minced fresh garlic

4 tablespoons dried parsley

2 (8-ounce) blocks cream cheese, cubed

4 (14.5-ounce) cans green beans, drained

2 (14.5-ounce) cans sliced carrots, drained

1 (12-ounce) bag frozen peas

1 (22.6-ounce) can condensed cream of mushroom soup

4 cups shredded medium Cheddar cheese

1 (32-ounce) bag frozen Tater Tots

Steps:

1. In a 17" round cast iron pan, combine beef, pepper, garlic salt, minced onion, minced garlic, and parsley and cook over medium-high heat for 15 minutes or until meat is cooked through, stirring occasionally.

2. Reduce heat to low and stir in cream cheese. Simmer until cheese is completely melted, about 15 minutes, stirring occasionally.

3. While cheese is melting, preheat oven to 375°F.

4. Stir in green beans, carrots, peas, and soup and continue cooking for an additional 10 minutes, stirring occasionally.

5. Top mixture with Cheddar, making sure to spread it out evenly. Then top cheese layer with Tater Tots.

6. Bake for 45 minutes or until Tater Tots are golden brown. Serve.

CHAPTER 2

Grilling and Barbecue Recipes

~ ✳ ~

She met a hardworking farm boy named
Luke who was raised on a dairy farm and
was a master at the grill.

When I met my husband years ago, I knew right away that he was different from what I imagined my future husband would be. He loved to fish and hunt, and every single Sunday his family would have a barbecue on the beach, and he would be in charge of grilling because he cooked the most perfect burgers and steaks ever. That was his thing: grilling meat, fish, and veggies. To him there wasn't anything you couldn't cook on a grill.

This farm boy who loved the outdoors and was the grill master threw me for a loop because I thought I had every part of my life all figured out. I knew where I would live, who I would marry, what I wanted to be when I grew up, how many children I would have, and even what their names would be. I knew what I wanted. But little did I know then that my soon-to-be husband, Luke, would forever change this city girl's heart.

When I moved to Michigan at twenty-one years old, I had no intention of settling down with anyone until I finished medical school and became a pediatrician. The one thing I did know is that I wasn't about to settle for a regular ole boy who lived on a dairy farm. No way! However, God had different plans for my future. One night I went to our church hockey game and there he was...this boy named Luke Bell, who had just finished shooting a goal. Immediately I was taken aback, and I started thinking that maybe I could *slightly* adjust my plans. Coincidently, that same night he also noticed me and told his best friend, "You see that girl with the blonde hair—I'm going to marry her." Shortly after, I invited him to come over for a game night at my house. Within four months of our first date, I realized that I wanted to be with him forever and decided that being a wife and mom was okay too.

Luke was raised on a dairy farm and is one of the hardest workers I have ever met. One thing that drew me to him was that he loved his mother so much and did whatever he could to help her out. His mother would prepare these huge meals not only for the family, but also for the others who helped on the farm all summer with cutting and baling hay. Their favorite meal was when she would make burgers on the grill. She'd load the burgers up with cheese and veggies, wrap them in tinfoil, pack everything into her Bronco, and head to the fields. This was something I had never seen before; she would make huge casseroles and pack them into her car and head out to the fields to feed a hungry, hardworking crew. I was completely impressed because she would do this every single day all summer long. She could put together these comfort-style meals in minutes, with huge portions that were filling but easy to make. She had the biggest cooking pans and casserole dishes I had ever seen. Like my mother, she also grew a huge garden and canned vegetables, salsas, and relishes. It was another way of providing for a big family, by having fresh foods at mealtime and storing some for the winter months.

My husband asked me to marry him on April Fool's Day of all days to pick. That next year we were married, and now it was time for me to not only make the meals that my mother made growing up but also try

Luke's mother's way of cooking. Looking back, I'm thankful that God showed me a different path and that I married the love of my life. I was super excited to have a kitchen of my own that I could start creating meals for my husband and soon-to-be family.

Luke was raised to enjoy the outdoors and live off the land. He took every opportunity to grab fish he caught or beef he raised to grill for his family to help make his mother's load lighter. Honestly, I never thought to use a grill, so I made burgers on my cooktop and broiled steaks in the oven. Luke shared with me different kinds of spices that pair great with beef, pork, and fish and taught me that when you cook on a grill, the temperature and cook times have to be adjusted compared to cooking in a kitchen. I learned a lot from my husband, and it opened a whole new world of preparing meals.

It just makes sense to devote this chapter on grilling and barbecue recipes to my husband, who is the best at showing his many cooking skills when it comes to grilling. When summer comes, the oven is pretty much shut down and our two grills are cleaned and ready to cook dinner for our big family. 🌹

Roasted Chicken *and* Veggie Medley

Sometimes when I don't really feel like cooking with lots of ingredients, I will just grab a whole chicken out of the fridge and slow cook it and serve with veggies. It's nice because you can throw it all into one pot and let it cook all day while you get some overdue housework done. You can also cook a bigger chicken and plan on using the leftovers for the next day. Some great ideas are shredding the chicken for tacos or pulled chicken barbecue sandwiches. This chicken also freezes well for future meals.

Prep Time: 30 minutes
Cook Time: 2 hours and **45** minutes
Yields: 10 servings

Chicken Ingredients:

1 (5-pound) whole chicken, innards removed

2 tablespoons smoked paprika

3 teaspoons each of garlic powder, onion powder, dried parsley, dried thyme, and kosher salt

2 teaspoons ground black pepper

1/2 teaspoon ground ginger

1/4 cup olive oil (or avocado oil)

3 tablespoons minced fresh garlic

Veggie Medley Ingredients:

2 medium zucchini, diced

2 medium summer squash, diced

12 medium carrots, peeled and diced

2 medium yellow onions, peeled and diced

2 medium red bell peppers, seeded and sliced

1 medium head broccoli, stem removed, diced

1 tablespoon dried thyme

1 tablespoon salt

1/2 tablespoon ground black pepper

2 tablespoons minced fresh garlic

2 tablespoons lemon zest

1/2 cup salted butter

Steps:

1. Preheat oven to 325°F.

2. In a roaster pan place whole chicken plus 1" water. In a medium bowl, combine paprika, garlic powder, onion powder, parsley, thyme, salt, pepper, and ginger and whisk together. Rub chicken with oil and minced garlic and then with seasoning mixture. Cover pan with tinfoil and bake until temperature of chicken reaches 165°F in thickest part of the thigh, about 2 hours.

3. When desired temperature is reached, turn off oven and let chicken cook another 15 minutes. Remove from oven and let it stand covered for 10 minutes. Transfer chicken to a cutting board. Pour the drippings from the roasting pan into a medium saucepan. Add Veggie Medley ingredients and stir.

4. Cook over medium heat for 20 minutes, stirring occasionally. Carve chicken and serve with veggies.

Noah's Burgers *with* Aioli Sauce

I was completely impressed with this recipe when Noah made it, and I added it to my saved recipes for future use. The first time he made these it was winter, so we cooked them inside, but they are also great on the grill! Noah spent all day searching out recipes and how to put different spices together. He did a terrific job on these burgers, and he wouldn't let me help him. He also made a fresh broccoli salad that went perfectly with his amazing burgers. Feel free to top these burgers with lettuce and tomato or whatever toppings you like!

Prep Time: 20 minutes
Cook Time: 25 minutes
Yields: 12 servings

Aioli Sauce Ingredients:

2 cups mayonnaise

4 tablespoons lemon juice

2 teaspoons lemon zest

1 teaspoon ground white pepper

2 teaspoons dried parsley

4 tablespoons minced fresh garlic

Burger Ingredients:

3 pounds 90/10 lean ground beef

1 pound ground pork sausage

2 tablespoons olive oil

2 tablespoons Dijon mustard

2 tablespoons dried thyme

2 tablespoons dried minced onion

2 teaspoons salt

2 teaspoons ground white pepper

1 (8-ounce) package sliced Swiss cheese

12 large eggs (1 large egg per burger)

12 onion-topped hamburger buns

Steps:

1. **Make the Aioli Sauce:** Combine mayo, lemon juice, lemon zest, pepper, parsley, and garlic in a medium bowl. Whisk together. Set aside.

2. **Make the Burgers:** In a large bowl, combine beef, pork, oil, mustard, thyme, minced onion, salt, and pepper. Mix together and form 12 burger patties.

3. Place burger patties into a large skillet over medium heat. Cook completely through, about 15 minutes, turning once. Top each burger with a cheese slice. Allow cheese to melt and remove burgers from pan.

4. In the same skillet over medium-low heat, fry each egg to your liking, then place 1 egg on top of each cooked burger.

5. Place burger patties on bottom buns, spread Aioli Sauce on bottom of top bun, and then top the burger with it. Serve.

BBQ Brisket Sliders

Sliders are kinda my thing—they are like mini dinners on a bun. And they work great with brisket. I like to cook a big roast so I can stretch two or three meals out of it. Briskets are pretty easy to make: Just choose your spices, dump, and go. You can slow cook it in the oven, on the grill, or smoke it, which is my husband's favorite way of cooking anything and everything. These sliders are not only great for dinner but also for lunchtime.

Prep Time: 30 minutes
Cook Time: 3 hours and **35** minutes
Yields: 12 servings

Ingredients:

1 (6-pound) beef chuck roast

3 large yellow onions, peeled and sliced

1 tablespoon ground white pepper

1 tablespoon ground yellow mustard

1 tablespoon salt

2 tablespoons applewood seasoning

3 tablespoons olive oil

2 (12-count) packages Hawaiian sweet rolls

1 cup plus 1 tablespoon Dijon mustard, divided

1 cup barbecue sauce

4 cups shredded medium Cheddar cheese

½ cup salted butter, melted

1 tablespoon dried minced onion

Steps:

1. In a large slow cooker, add roast, onions, pepper, ground mustard, salt, applewood seasoning, and oil. Cover and cook on high for 2–4 hours or until brisket is tender and easily shredded.

2. Once brisket is cooked, pull out of slow cooker, shred, and set aside.

3. Preheat oven to 375°F.

4. Place rolls on ungreased 18" × 26" baking sheets. Cut each roll in half horizontally and spread 1 cup Dijon mustard on bottom. Add a generous amount of shredded brisket, and brush on barbecue sauce. Sprinkle with cheese and return tops of rolls.

5. In a small bowl, combine melted butter, minced onion, and remaining 1 tablespoon Dijon mustard. Whisk together and brush over tops of rolls.

6. Bake for 35 minutes. Serve.

Brisket Waffle Bowls Topped *with* Mashed Potatoes

This recipe is so fun to make. The sweetness of the waffle bowl paired with the saltiness of the brisket works out just perfectly. My husband, Luke, is a master at the smoker, and he usually slow cooks the brisket for this all day until the meat is juicy and almost falling off the bone! Our family loves ice cream so much, and this recipe was like eating an ice cream sundae but with our favorite dinner ingredients. Can you get any better than a warm waffle bowl filled with creamy mashed potatoes and topped with yummy goodness? I think not!

Prep Time: **30** minutes

Cook Time: **3** hours and **25** minutes

Yields: **10** servings

Ingredients:

1 (5-pound) beef chuck roast

2 tablespoons minced fresh garlic

2 tablespoons dried minced onion

4 tablespoons applewood seasoning

1 tablespoon garlic powder

1 tablespoon ground white pepper

1 tablespoon garlic salt

1 cup water

1 (5-pound) bag yellow potatoes, cut into cubes

1 cup salted butter

1 tablespoon salt

1 tablespoon ground black pepper

1 (10-count) package large waffle bowls

4 cups finely shredded medium Cheddar cheese

1 (16-ounce) package bacon, cooked and chopped

1 (16-ounce) jar pickled red onions

Steps:

1. Place roast into a slow cooker and cover with seasonings. Add water and put lid on. Cook over low heat for 3 hours or until meat pulls apart easily.

2. Fill a 6-quart saucepot with water and add potatoes. Let boil for 15 minutes or until potatoes are soft. Remove from heat, drain, and add butter, salt, and pepper. Whip with a hand mixer and set aside.

3. Remove roast from juices and shred with a fork.

4. Preheat oven to 375°F.

5. Fill waffle bowls with mashed potatoes, brisket, cheese, and cooked bacon. Place on an ungreased 18" × 26" baking sheet. Warm filled waffle bowls in the oven for 5–10 minutes, remove, and top with pickled onions. Serve.

Cast Iron Cowboy Beans

This is one of the recipes that I make often, especially in the fall. When I make it using my cast iron Dutch oven, I always think of the cowboys years ago and how they cooked over a bonfire at night under the stars. This can be a complete main dish or omit the ground beef and brats to serve the beans as a side dish, with a nice juicy medium rare steak hot off the grill. Complete this meal with corn bread, and it's the perfect cowboy-themed dinner.

Prep Time: 30 minutes
Cook Time: 1 hour and **5** minutes
Yields: 12–14 servings

Ingredients:

1 (16-ounce) package bacon, chopped
1 tablespoon minced fresh garlic
1 large yellow onion, peeled and chopped
2 pounds 90/10 lean ground beef
1 tablespoon garlic salt
1 tablespoon garlic powder
2 tablespoons liquid aminos (or soy sauce)
2 tablespoons Worcestershire sauce
1 cup packed light brown sugar
2 tablespoons Dijon mustard
1 cup molasses
¼ cup ketchup
2 (8-count) packages cheesy brats, sliced
1 (28-ounce) can crushed tomatoes
1 (29-ounce) can kidney beans
1 (28-ounce) can original baked beans
1 (28-ounce) can tomato sauce

Steps:

1. In an 8-quart cast iron Dutch oven on the stovetop, combine bacon, minced garlic, and onion. Cook, stirring often, over medium heat for 10 minutes.

2. Add beef, garlic salt, and garlic powder. Cook an additional 15 minutes, stirring occasionally.

3. Preheat oven to 375°F.

4. Add liquid aminos, Worcestershire sauce, sugar, mustard, molasses, and ketchup. Mix together and continue cooking over medium heat for 10 minutes or until meat is cooked through, stirring as needed.

5. Add brats, crushed tomatoes, beans, and tomato sauce. Stir together, place top on Dutch oven, and cook for an additional 30 minutes in the oven. Serve.

Homemade Potato Salad

My husband's all-time favorite dish is hands down potato salad, which goes great with any cookout. If he could eat potato salad for every meal he definitely would—that's how much he likes my Homemade Potato Salad. Over the years I have slowly added more ingredients to add some pizzazz. I grow tons of zucchini in my garden every year, and I make a terrific sweet zucchini relish that I occasionally add to this salad in place of the sweet relish.

Prep Time: 20 minutes
Cook Time: 15 minutes
Yields: 10 servings

Ingredients:

1 (5-pound) bag Yukon Gold potatoes, chopped
2 cups pitted and chopped green olives
2 cups cubed medium Cheddar cheese
6 medium green onions, ends trimmed, chopped
12 ounces bacon, cooked, cooled, and chopped
4 cups mayonnaise
2 tablespoons Dijon mustard
3 tablespoons sweet relish
12 large eggs, hard-boiled, peeled, cooled, and sliced
1 tablespoon salt
½ tablespoon ground black pepper

Steps:

1. Place potatoes in a large saucepan or stockpot and cover with water. Boil 10–15 minutes until just soft when poked with a fork. Drain and transfer to a large bowl. Let them cool in the fridge for 30 minutes or until completely cooled.

2. Add remaining ingredients to the potatoes and mix well. Cover and store in the fridge until ready to serve.

Grilled Asparagus Wrapped in Bacon *with* Ranch Corn on the Cob

When summer finally hits up north, we get our grill and smoker ready for the season. We grow our own asparagus, and I just can't wait to harvest it and use it in this amazing recipe. We also definitely look forward to corn on the cob every summer, and this ranch recipe adds so much flavor. Both of these sides go great with burgers or steak on the grill, and both are great ideas for adding veggies to a meal rather than the typical fries.

Prep Time: 30 minutes
Cook Time: 35 minutes
Yields: 12 servings

Asparagus Ingredients:

1 cup packed light brown sugar
½ tablespoon ground black pepper
1 tablespoon minced fresh garlic
½ cup salted butter
1 (16-ounce) package bacon, uncooked
2 bunches (18 spears per bunch) asparagus, ends trimmed

Corn on the Cob Ingredients:

2 (1-ounce) packets dry ranch seasoning mix
1 tablespoon dried parsley
½ tablespoon ground white pepper
½ tablespoon garlic salt
½ cup salted butter, sliced into 1" sections
12 large ears corn, shucked and rinsed

Steps:

1. Preheat grill to 350°F and line the grates with tinfoil.

2. **Make the Asparagus:** In a small saucepan, combine sugar, black pepper, minced garlic, and ½ cup butter. Cook on stovetop over low heat until completely melted, about 10 minutes, stirring occasionally. Remove saucepan from heat and add uncooked bacon to pan, coating it well.

3. Take 4 spears of asparagus and wrap tightly with 1 piece of bacon. Continue with groups of 4 until all are wrapped tightly around with bacon. Set aside.

4. **Make the Corn on the Cob:** In a medium bowl, combine ranch seasoning, parsley, white pepper, and garlic salt. Whisk together and set aside.

5. Place asparagus on one side of grill. Cook for 10 minutes, turning occasionally or until bacon is crispy.

6. On the other side of grill, lay down slices of butter and then lay corn on top. Rotate corn as it cooks. Once completely covered in butter, sprinkle with ranch mixture. Corn will take about 15 minutes to cook until done. Serve.

Campfire All-in-One Burger Meal

When I was younger, every summer our big family would go camping, and I knew that my dad was going to make his burger meal. It just wouldn't be the same if my dad didn't make these. I thought it was super cool to be outside under the stars and eating dinner. I grew up in a family of ten myself, and my parents always made sure to find easy recipes for our nightly cookouts that were special and only for our camping adventures.

Prep Time: 15 minutes
Cook Time: 20 minutes
Yields: 10 servings

Ingredients:

5 pounds 90/10 lean ground beef
2 tablespoons dried minced onion
2 tablespoons minced fresh garlic
1 tablespoon salt
$\frac{1}{2}$ tablespoon ground black pepper
8 large Yukon Gold potatoes, sliced thin horizontally
4 large sweet Vidalia onions, peeled and sliced thick
5 large tomatoes, sliced
$\frac{1}{2}$ cup salted butter, sliced thin

Steps:

1. In a large bowl, combine beef and seasonings. Mix well and form into 10 burger patties.

2. Place a piece of tinfoil down and layer with 1 slice of potato, 1 slice of onion, burger patty, 1 slice of tomato, and another slice of onion and potato. Top with 2 pats of butter and fold foil over the top and seal. Repeat for other 9 burgers.

3. Place on a campfire grate and cook for 20 minutes or until burger patties are cooked through and potatoes are soft but not mushy. Serve.

The "Gideon Special" Burger

Whenever my son Gideon walks into the kitchen, I know the food is going to be unique and super good. His favorite type of cooking is to grill fish and burgers. He is great at just grabbing whatever he finds in the fridge and pantry and creating a masterpiece. This burger definitely put him on the map, and it's a family recipe keeper. I love it when my kids just walk into the kitchen and make an entire meal for our big family. Plus, it gives this mama a day off from the kitchen.

Prep Time: 20 minutes
Cook Time: 30 minutes
Yields: 10 servings

Ingredients:

4 pounds 90/10 lean ground beef

1 tablespoon salt

$\frac{1}{2}$ tablespoon ground black pepper

2 (8-ounce) packages medium Cheddar cheese slices

1 cup salted butter

2 large yellow onions, peeled and sliced

1 (16-ounce) package whole portobello mushrooms, sliced

$\frac{1}{2}$ cup olive oil

1 (26-ounce) bag frozen shredded hash browns

20 slices white bread, toasted

1 head iceberg lettuce, sliced

4 large tomatoes, sliced

1 cup mayonnaise

1 cup barbecue sauce

Steps:

1. In a large bowl, combine beef, salt, and pepper and then make 10 burger patties. Cook on a griddle over medium heat for 10 minutes, flipping halfway through the cooking time. Turn off burner and place 2 cheese slices on each burger patty. Let stand.

2. In a large skillet, combine butter, onion, and mushrooms. Cook over medium heat for 10 minutes or until veggies are tender, stirring occasionally. Remove veggies from pan. Set aside.

3. Heat 1 tablespoon oil in the pan over medium heat. Form 10 rough patties with shredded hash browns and place 3 to 4 in the pan and cook until browned, flip, and continue cooking until both sides are browned, about 10 minutes total. Repeat with remaining oil and hash browns.

4. Construct the burgers by taking one piece toasted bread and layering on it a burger, a hash brown patty, onion and mushroom mixture, lettuce, tomato, mayo, barbecue sauce, and then a toasted bread top. Repeat with remaining ingredients. Serve.

Noah's Pulled Pork *and* Beans Sliders

Every Sunday afternoon I make brunch using different kinds of slider rolls. I have yet to find a food that doesn't go great with these sweet rolls. And I make baked beans often, no matter the season, because they go with any main dish. My son Noah came up with this great idea to combine leftover baked beans with pulled pork and slider rolls into one dinner.

Prep Time: 30 minutes
Cook Time: 4 hours
Yields: 10 servings

Pork Ingredients:

1 (4-pound) pork shoulder

1 tablespoon minced fresh garlic

2 tablespoons applewood seasoning

1 tablespoon Worcestershire sauce

2 tablespoons dried minced onion

2 large yellow onions, peeled and sliced thin

1 cup water

Beans Ingredients:

2 (16-ounce) cans original baked beans

1 tablespoon packed light brown sugar

¼ cup molasses

1 tablespoon each of minced fresh garlic, Dijon mustard, salt, and ground white pepper

Additional Ingredients:

2 (12-count) packages Hawaiian sweet rolls

1 cup barbecue sauce

4 cups shredded medium Cheddar cheese

1 cup salted butter, melted

2 tablespoons dried parsley

2 tablespoons Dijon mustard

1 tablespoon sesame seeds

Steps:

1. Preheat oven to 300°F.

2. **Make the Pork:** Place pork, seasonings, onion, and water in a roaster pan. Cover with tinfoil and cook for 3 hours or until pork is easily shredded. Remove from oven and shred meat. Set aside.

3. **Make the Beans:** In a medium saucepan, combine Beans ingredients. Mix well and cook over low heat for 30 minutes, stirring occasionally.

4. Increase oven temperature to 375°F.

5. Place rolls on ungreased 18" × 26" baking sheets. Cut each loaf in half horizontally and layer the bottoms with barbecue sauce, pulled pork, onions from roaster pan, beans, and cheese. Place tops on.

6. In a small bowl, combine butter, parsley, and mustard. Mix well and brush over tops of rolls. Sprinkle with sesame seeds. Bake at 375°F for 30 minutes. Serve.

Blue Cheese–Stuffed Burgers

What's better than a juicy burger? How about one stuffed with different kinds of cheese. This was the second meal I made for Luke after we were first married. He loves burgers and I love blue cheese, so I knew this was a recipe that we both would enjoy. I'd hoped that if I made this burger, it would knock his socks off. Well, he loved it, and I sealed the deal with my Homemade Potato Salad. Two of his favorites on the same plate made it a great start to our marriage.

Prep Time: 30 minutes
Cook Time: 20 minutes
Yields: 16 servings

Ingredients:

4 pounds 90/10 lean ground beef

1 tablespoon plus 1 teaspoon salt, divided

1 tablespoon plus 1 teaspoon ground black pepper, divided

1 tablespoon ground yellow mustard

2 tablespoons minced fresh garlic

2 tablespoons dried minced onion

4 tablespoons Dijon mustard

1 cup crumbled blue cheese

2 (8-ounce) blocks cream cheese, softened

2 (8-count) packages onion-topped hamburger buns

6 cups sliced portobello mushrooms

2 large yellow onions, peeled and sliced

4 tablespoons Worcestershire sauce

3 large tomatoes, sliced

1 cup mayonnaise

1 cup dill relish

Steps:

1. In a large bowl, combine beef, 1 tablespoon each of salt and pepper, ground mustard, garlic, and minced onion. Mix well and form into 32 patties, about ¼"-thick.

2. In a small bowl, combine Dijon mustard, blue cheese, and cream cheese. Place 2 tablespoons cheese mixture on top of each of 16 patties. Top with remaining 16 patties and seal edges.

3. In a large skillet, cook burger patties over medium heat for 12 minutes, turning once. Place burger patties on bottom bun.

4. To the drippings in the pan, add mushrooms, onions, remaining 1 teaspoon each of salt and pepper, and Worcestershire sauce. Cook over medium-high heat for 5 minutes or until veggies are tender, stirring occasionally.

5. Top burgers with mushrooms and onions, tomatoes, mayo, and relish, then finish with top bun. Serve.

CHAPTER 3

Breakfast Recipes

~ ✳ ~

They tried to have a family with no success and after four years adopted their first son David, whose favorite meal was breakfast.

David was my morning boy when he was younger and was always ready for breakfast. It was his favorite meal of the day, especially when it included bacon. How do I know that? Because at the end of one day I noticed his cheeks were chubbier than normal, and sure enough he had bacon stored on each side. It was amazing to me that he could go all day with food still sitting in his cheeks! He loved mornings, and, no matter if he was crawling or had started walking, he would make his way to the kitchen, grab a fork or spoon, and sit in his spot at the table. He'd swing his little legs and look at me patiently with a huge smile and a milk mustache on his face as he waited for breakfast.

David was such a blessing to Luke and me because he fulfilled that yearning we had to become parents. After four long years of trying to get pregnant with no success, we decided to take a huge step of faith and explore adoption. We were not very confident in that decision at first because it was a whole new area in life that we weren't sure we were ready for and had no idea where to even start. Would we love an adopted child the same as one that was biological? Would that child's birth families accept us and be open to us in their families? There were so many questions, but we made the call and went to the classes and made a scrapbook showing our lives, hobbies, families, and why we wanted to adopt a child. The hardest part was having to write a letter to the birth mom telling her why she should choose us to adopt her baby. I think I cried the entire time writing my letter. Then we just had to wait and hope a birth mom would choose us and trust that we would love her baby as much as she does.

Right before we got the call that would forever change our lives, we both decided that we would call the agency to let them know we were having second thoughts, but instead our phone rang with the news that a birth mom wanted to meet us. We met with David's birth mom, and she was amazing and gave me the best hug I ever had in my entire life. I melted in her arms; here I thought we would be a support for her, but it was the other way around. That hug made me feel like everything was going to be okay, and you know what? It was.

David was born three months later, and it was one of the best moments of my life. His birth mom gave me the best gift: motherhood. She chose us to raise her son, and today we are friends and she is one of the strongest women I know. What courage it took for her to willingly give her son up for adoption. I will be forever grateful to her for letting me also be a mother to David. As a first-time mother I had the support of not only Luke and our families, but also David's entire birth family. We chose to keep his adoption open because we knew that his family needed him just as much as we needed them to support us as David grew up. We wanted them to be a part of every milestone in his life.

Now I was not only a wife, but a mother to a son too. Let me tell you, David was my first challenge with cooking because he was a super picky eater as he grew up—except at breakfast time—and I had to be very inventive when making meals for the three of us. He challenged my cooking skills in every way possible, but I was up for the task. Those more sophisticated and impressive meals I made for my husband turned into simple, kid-friendly, family style meals like mac and cheese with hot dogs or tomato soup and grilled cheese. He wasn't the biggest fan of vegetables, but there was one meal I knew I could fall back on when I was at my wit's end trying to cook something he would gobble up—breakfast. And to this day he will come downstairs with that amazing smile to the kitchen, take a big whiff, and guess what's for breakfast. Then he grabs the milk and chocolate syrup, gives me a big hug, sits down at the counter, and watches me with a fork in his hand—this time with a grown-up milk mustache—as he patiently waits for the food to be done.

The recipes in this chapter are dedicated to David and his love of all things breakfast. Whenever I ask my children what they would like for our weekly menu, he always answers with the same meal: Homemade Buttermilk Biscuits and Gravy. When no one is looking, I will put some aside in a container and hide it in the back of the fridge so David can enjoy it the next couple of days. Sometimes it makes it to the next day, but most of the time I see him eating it at night for snack time with the same big smile. One thing that brings so much happiness to my heart is how every single time before he leaves the kitchen, he makes sure to give me an extra big hug with a thank you followed by an "I love you, Mom." 🌹

Homemade Buttermilk Biscuits *and* Gravy

Growing up, my father made his special biscuits and gravy often. We just loved eating breakfast for dinner; it was one of my favorite meals ever. Now my family also looks forward to when I make these Homemade Buttermilk Biscuits and Gravy. This biscuit recipe is so easy to make and absolutely amazing. My son David likes to sleep in, but when he knows I'm making biscuits and gravy he's downstairs the minute he smells breakfast cooking.

Prep Time: 30 minutes
Cook Time: 45 minutes
Yields: 10 servings

Sausage Gravy Ingredients:

3 pounds ground pork
$3/4$ cup salted butter, divided
$1/2$ teaspoon crushed red pepper flakes
1 teaspoon ground black pepper, divided
$1 1/2$ teaspoons garlic powder, divided
1 tablespoon dried minced onion
1 cup all-purpose flour
1 teaspoon garlic salt
2 cups heavy cream
4 cups whole milk

Biscuit Ingredients:

$3 1/3$ cups all-purpose flour
$1 1/2$ cups buttermilk
1 tablespoon plus 1 teaspoon baking powder
1 teaspoon each of salt, ground black pepper, and garlic powder
$1/2$ cup salted butter, softened

Steps:

1. **Make the Sausage Gravy:** In a large skillet, combine pork, $1/4$ cup butter, red pepper, $1/2$ teaspoon black pepper, 1 teaspoon garlic powder, and minced onion. Cook over medium heat for 15 minutes or until meat is cooked through, stirring occasionally. Remove meat with a slotted spoon and set aside, reserving the drippings in the pan.

2. To the drippings, add remaining $1/2$ cup butter, flour, garlic salt, and remaining $1/2$ teaspoon each of black pepper and garlic powder. Cook over medium heat while whisking until it forms a paste, about 2 minutes. Let simmer for 1 minute and slowly add cream and then milk, whisking constantly. Reduce heat to low and continue whisking until thickened, about 10 minutes. Return meat to pan and mix well. Set aside.

3. Preheat oven to 375°F.

4. **Make the Biscuits:** In a bowl, combine all Biscuit ingredients and mix well. Remove dough from bowl and place on a floured surface. Knead six to seven times, then roll out dough about $1/4$" thick and cut with a round 4" cookie cutter or glass bowl.

5. Place biscuits on an 18" × 26" baking sheet lined with parchment paper and bake for 15 minutes. Serve biscuits with Sausage Gravy on top.

Gideon's Favorite "Mom's Breakfast Pizza"

One morning, I wanted to make something special for breakfast and decided to put together a breakfast pizza. Normally, you don't see gravy included on a pizza, but I knew that my homemade sausage gravy would be amazing on this. That morning, all my children got up early because they were super excited for breakfast, and Gideon looked at me and said, "Mom, this is the best breakfast meal you have ever made." He grabbed extras and hid them to eat the next two mornings.

Prep Time: 30 minutes
Cook Time: 55 minutes
Yields: 12 servings

Ingredients:

4 (8-ounce) tubes refrigerated crescent rolls

2 pounds ground breakfast sausage

$\frac{1}{2}$ cup salted butter

1 cup all-purpose flour

1 tablespoon salt

1 tablespoon ground black pepper

2 cups heavy cream

4 cups whole milk

4 cups shredded medium Cheddar cheese

24 large eggs, cooked scrambled

2 (16-ounce) packages bacon, cooked and chopped

1 (16-ounce) package deli smoked ham, chopped

Steps:

1. Preheat oven to 375°F.

2. On 2 ungreased 18" × 26" baking sheets, roll out and flatten crescent rolls, creating a large pizza crust on each pan. Bake for 10 minutes and then remove from oven and set aside.

3. In a large saucepan, cook sausage over medium heat until done, about 15 minutes, stirring occasionally. Remove sausage with a slotted spoon and set aside, reserving the drippings in the pan.

4. To the drippings in pan, add butter, flour, salt, and pepper. Whisk until a paste forms, about 2 minutes, and then let simmer for 2 more minutes.

5. Slowly whisk in cream, continuing to stir, then slowly add milk. Reduce heat to low and whisk until cream thickens, about 5 minutes. Return sausage to pan and stir.

6. Top each crust with 1 cup cheese, then $\frac{1}{4}$ of the sausage gravy. Layer scrambled eggs, bacon, and ham over each pizza. Top with remaining sausage gravy and remaining cheese.

7. Bake for 20 minutes. Serve.

Breakfast Potpie

Our family loves chicken potpie, and I knew I had to try that recipe for breakfast in some way. My kids were so excited about this recipe that they hung out in the kitchen just watching me the entire time. I cooked on convection mode because it cooks not only the tops but also the bottoms to make sure the biscuits are cooked completely. The potpie is so creamy with these flaky biscuits.

Prep Time: 30 minutes
Cook Time: 1 hour and **20** minutes
Yields: 10–12 servings

Ingredients:

24 large eggs, beaten
2 tablespoons avocado oil
2 pounds ground pork
1 tablespoon onion powder
1 tablespoon dried parsley
1 tablespoon minced fresh garlic
3/4 cup salted butter, divided
1 cup all-purpose flour
1 teaspoon salt
1 teaspoon ground black pepper
1/2 teaspoon cayenne pepper
3 1/2 cups cold whole milk
3 (8-count) tubes original Grands! Biscuits
2 cups shredded medium Cheddar cheese

Steps:

1. Preheat oven to 375°F.

2. In a large skillet coated in oil, cook eggs for 10 minutes over medium heat or until almost done. Set aside.

3. In a large saucepan, combine pork, onion powder, parsley, and garlic. Cook over medium heat for 15 minutes or until pork is cooked through, stirring occasionally. Remove pork from pan and set aside, reserving drippings in the pan.

4. To the drippings, add 1/2 cup butter, flour, salt, and peppers. Cook over medium heat while whisking. Once a paste forms, about 2 minutes, let it simmer for 1 minute.

5. Slowly add milk. Continue whisking until gravy thickens, about 5 minutes. Add cooked sausage and eggs to the pan and stir well.

6. Grease the bottom of a 10" × 15" casserole dish. Flatten 12 biscuits and place on the bottom and press down again.

7. Layer with egg and sausage mixture, cheese, and top with the other 12 biscuits, flattened.

8. Melt remaining 1/4 cup butter in the microwave, about 1 minute, and brush over biscuits. Bake for 45 minutes or until biscuits are completely cooked through. Serve.

Breakfast Pasties

We live way, way, way up north in the upper peninsula of Michigan—an area known for the best pasties. The traditional pasty has beef, potatoes, carrots, and rutabaga and is served with ketchup. These breakfast pasties have some of the best breakfast items inside. I used Italian sausage because it reminded me of cudighi, a spicy sausage that we mix with beef to make burgers, another food we "Yoopers" are famous for.

Prep Time: 30 minutes
Cook Time: 1 hour
Yields: 10 servings

Ingredients:

2 tablespoons avocado oil (or olive oil)

24 large eggs, beaten

2½ pounds ground Italian sausage

4 (2.75-ounce) packets peppered gravy mix

2 (2-count) boxes refrigerated premade store-bought pie crusts

4 tablespoons all-purpose flour

1 (16-ounce) package bacon, cooked and chopped

4 cups shredded medium Cheddar cheese

4 tablespoons salted butter, melted

Steps:

1. Coat a large pan in oil and place over medium heat. Add eggs and scramble until almost done, around 10 minutes, stirring as needed. Set aside.

2. In a medium saucepan, cook sausage over medium heat for 15 minutes or until cooked through, stirring occasionally. Set aside.

3. In a separate medium saucepan, make gravy according to packet directions and simmer over low heat for 10 minutes. Remove from heat and add sausage to gravy. Mix well to combine and then divide into two equal portions and set both aside.

4. Preheat oven to 375°F.

5. Roll out pie crusts on a floured surface. Cut each crust into four equal squares.

6. To one half of each crust, layer on eggs, 1 portion of sausage gravy mixture, bacon, and cheese. Fold the crust in half over filling and roll the edges over to seal or seal edges with a fork. Place the pasties on ungreased 18" × 26" baking sheets. Brush the tops with the melted butter and then bake for 20 minutes. Serve with remaining portion of gravy.

French Onion Hash Brown Casserole

This is a family recipe that my big sister, Carey, shared with me. My kids went crazy over this recipe when she made it for us. They had me make it the next day (with the guidance of my big sis) because they loved it so much. I made sure to double the recipe, and we pretty much ate it all week for breakfast. The flavors in this dish are amazing, and when we came home from visiting her, my kids told Luke all about it, and I had to make it again for him to try.

Prep Time: 30 minutes
Cook Time: 1 hour
Yields: 10 servings

Ingredients:

2 pounds ground breakfast sausage

1 large yellow onion, peeled and chopped

1 tablespoon minced fresh garlic

2 (8-ounce) containers sour cream

1 (10.5-ounce) can condensed cream of chicken soup

1 (16-ounce) container French onion dip

4 cups shredded medium Cheddar cheese, divided

1 (14-count) package pork sausage links, cooked and sliced

1 (32-ounce) bag frozen shredded hash browns

Steps:

1. Preheat oven to 375°F.

2. Combine ground sausage, onion, and garlic in a large skillet and cook for 15 minutes over medium heat, stirring occasionally. Set aside.

3. In a large bowl, combine sour cream, soup, dip, 2 cups cheese, and sliced sausage links. Mix to combine and then remove 3 cups of mixture to reserve for top of casserole.

4. To the remaining sauce, add hash browns and mix well. Next, add cooked sausage mixture and stir again.

5. Pour mixture into 2 greased 9" × 13" casserole dishes, then pour reserved sauce mixture over top and spread evenly. Sprinkle with remaining 2 cups cheese and bake for 45 minutes. Serve.

Loaded Breakfast Sliders

Every Sunday after church, I like to make our big family a big breakfast. I have created almost fifty different slider meals, and I knew that I had to make a breakfast slider. Having six boys means that I often have to add lots of ingredients to my meals to make them more filling. I added every breakfast ingredient I could think of to these sliders. They are the perfect "grilled sandwich." The top is nice and crispy, and the inside is cheesy and stuffed full.

Prep Time: 30 minutes
Cook Time: 40 minutes
Yields: 12 servings

Ingredients:

2 pounds ground breakfast sausage
1/2 cup salted butter
1/2 tablespoon salt
1/2 tablespoon ground black pepper
1/2 cup all-purpose flour
2 cups heavy cream
2 cups whole milk
2 (12-count) packages Hawaiian sweet rolls
1 (16-ounce) package sliced black forest ham
2 (10-count) packages sliced provolone cheese
12 large eggs, scrambled soft
2 (10-count) packages sliced medium Cheddar cheese
1 (16-ounce) package bacon, cooked and crumbled
1/2 cup salted butter, melted
1 teaspoon garlic powder
1 teaspoon dried minced onion
1 teaspoon dried parsley

Steps:

1. In a medium saucepan, cook sausage over medium heat for 15 minutes or until cooked through, stirring occasionally. Remove sausage from pan and set aside, reserving drippings in the pan.

2. To the drippings, add 1/2 cup butter, salt, pepper, and flour. Whisk over medium heat until it forms a paste, about 2 minutes. Let simmer 1 minute, then slowly add cream and then milk, making sure to whisk continually.

3. Add sausage back to pan, stir to mix, and then set mixture aside.

4. Preheat oven to 350°F.

5. Place rolls on ungreased 18" × 26" baking sheets and cut each loaf in half horizontally. Remove top layer and layer bottom rolls with ham, provolone, scrambled eggs, Cheddar, bacon, and sausage mixture. Return tops.

6. In a small bowl combine melted butter, garlic powder, minced onion, and parsley. Whisk and then brush over the tops of rolls.

7. Bake for 20 minutes. Serve.

French Toast Sliders

French toast is one of my favorite breakfast foods to make for my family. It's a meal that is simple to make and tastes amazing. French toast and sausage are the perfect breakfast pairing, so I thought why not turn them into sliders! These French Toast Sliders are just the right size for dipping into warm Michigan maple syrup. For some more flavor, try adding pepper jack cheese and ham for a savory taste.

Prep Time: 25 minutes
Cook Time: 50 minutes
Yields: 12 servings

Ingredients:

36 large eggs, divided

3 pounds ground breakfast sausage

½ teaspoon ground ginger

½ teaspoon ground nutmeg

1 tablespoon ground cinnamon

1 cup vanilla-flavored creamer

2 (12-count) packages Hawaiian sweet rolls

2 (10-count) packages sliced medium Cheddar cheese

¼ cup pure maple syrup, plus 4 cups for dipping

3 tablespoons confectioners' sugar

Steps:

1. Preheat oven to 350°F.

2. In a large bowl, crack 24 eggs, whisk, and pour into a greased 18" × 26" baking sheet. Bake for 5 minutes or until eggs are cooked through. Remove and cut into large squares. Set aside.

3. Place sausage onto another greased 18" × 26" baking sheet. Press firmly and evenly on the sheet and bake for 15 minutes or until cooked through. Remove and cut into large squares. Set aside.

4. Combine remaining 12 eggs, ginger, nutmeg, cinnamon, and creamer in an ungreased 9" × 13" casserole dish and whisk together.

5. Cut both loaves of rolls in half horizontally and dip the top and bottom layer of each loaf into egg mixture, soaking both sides, then place on 2 ungreased 18" × 26" baking sheets. Bake for 20 minutes.

6. Layer bottom rolls with cooked eggs, sausage, and cheese slices. Place tops back on and brush tops with ¼ cup maple syrup. Bake for another 10 minutes to warm sliders up.

7. Remove sliders from the oven and sprinkle with sugar. Serve with maple syrup for dipping.

Breakfast Lasagna

My boys absolutely love lasagna for dinner. There isn't a week that goes by that they don't ask me to make my Cast Iron Lasagna. So why not try to make a Breakfast Lasagna? I used the same concept as my dinner lasagna but paired it with a creamy sausage filling, and we now have another successful breakfast recipe to add to the books.

Prep Time: 25 minutes
Cook Time: 1 hour and **5** minutes
Yields: 10–12 servings

Ingredients:

4 tablespoons avocado oil (or olive oil), divided

24 large eggs, beaten

4 pounds ground pork sausage

2 tablespoons minced fresh garlic

1 tablespoon each of garlic powder, dried parsley, and dried oregano

2 tablespoons dried minced onion

1 cup all-purpose flour

1 teaspoon salt

1 teaspoon ground black pepper

4 cups whole milk

3 cups shredded Parmesan cheese, divided

1 (8-ounce) container ricotta cheese

1 (8-ounce) container cottage cheese

2 (9-ounce) boxes oven-ready lasagna noodles

Steps:

1. Preheat oven to 375°F.

2. Heat 2 tablespoons oil in a large skillet and set over medium heat. Add eggs and scramble until soft, about 10 minutes, stirring occasionally. Set aside.

3. In a large saucepan, combine sausage, minced garlic, garlic powder, parsley, oregano, and minced onion and cook over medium heat for 15 minutes or until cooked through, stirring a few times. Remove sausage to a bowl with a slotted spoon and set aside, reserving drippings in the pan.

4. To the drippings in the pan, add flour, salt, and pepper. Whisk over medium heat until a paste forms, about 2 minutes. Let simmer 1 minute, then slowly add milk, continuing to whisk until gravy thickens, about 5 minutes. Remove half of the gravy and set aside. Return sausage to pan with the remaining gravy and add eggs. Mix together.

5. In a medium bowl, combine 1 cup Parmesan, ricotta, and cottage cheese.

6. In an ungreased 10" × 15" casserole dish, pour in 1 cup gravy, spreading along the bottom, then layer noodles, half the sausage mixture, noodles, 1 cup gravy, cheese mixture, noodles, the remaining sausage mixture, noodles, 2 cups gravy, and top with remaining 2 cups Parmesan. Bake for 30 minutes or until the noodles are soft. Serve.

Gideon's Greek Omelet

Gideon is quite the chef; he comes up with the best meals from simply grabbing odds and ends in the pantry and fridge. He can just walk into the kitchen without a plan on what he will cook, start pulling items to create a unique dish, and it always turns out great. He will grab foods that most people wouldn't think to combine together. This omelet is one of those dishes—he just started grabbing ingredients and putting them together in a kind of trial-and-error experiment. And the results are great!

Prep Time: 30 minutes
Cook Time: 10 minutes each
Yields: 10 servings

Ingredients:

24 large eggs

2 tablespoons heavy cream

1 teaspoon salt

½ teaspoon ground black pepper

3 tablespoons unsalted butter, divided

2 (10-ounce) packages cherry tomatoes, cut into halves

2 (8-ounce) jars sun-dried tomatoes, drained and diced

1 (10-ounce) package whole portobello mushrooms, diced

1 (16-ounce) package sliced black forest ham, chopped

4 cups chopped fresh spinach leaves

3 cups shredded Parmesan cheese

3 cups shredded Romano cheese

1 (24-ounce) container feta cheese

¼ cup dried basil, divided into 12 teaspoons

Steps:

1. In a medium bowl, whisk together eggs, cream, salt, and pepper.

2. Warm a large saucepan over medium heat, then reduce heat to low and grease the pan with 1 teaspoon butter. Pour in ½ cup egg mixture and cook until cooked through, slightly rotating pan to spread eggs over entire pan.

3. Layer one side of the omelet with both types of tomatoes, mushrooms, ham, spinach, Parmesan, and Romano. Fold omelet in half to cover ingredients. Top with 2 tablespoons feta (or more if desired) and 1 teaspoon basil.

4. Repeat with remaining 9 omelets. Serve garnished with feta and basil.

Cast Iron Hawaiian Breakfast Ring

My 17" cast iron pan gets used quite a bit. I have figured out how much I can put into this pan to feed my big family without overflowing. I actually had the pan for years before I finally started cooking with it. The size of it (and cast iron cooking in general) was intimidating for me to use because as a new cook I wasn't sure how to actually cook with it. Now I am constantly trying to create new recipes like this Hawaiian Breakfast Ring simply to use this amazing cast iron pan.

Prep Time: 30 minutes
Cook Time: 45 minutes
Yields: 10–12 servings

Ingredients:

2 pounds bacon, chopped

1 tablespoon ground black pepper

$\frac{1}{2}$ cup pure maple syrup

2 (8-ounce) tubes sweet Hawaiian crescent rolls

2 cups shredded Swiss cheese, divided

12 large eggs, scrambled and cooked soft

1 (16-ounce) package sliced black forest ham, chopped

$\frac{1}{2}$ cup salted butter, melted

2 teaspoons garlic salt

Steps:

1. In a large skillet, combine bacon, pepper, and maple syrup. Cook over medium heat for 15 minutes or until bacon is crispy and maple syrup has thickened. Set aside.

2. Preheat oven to 375°F.

3. In the middle of a 17" round cast iron pan, place a small bowl upside down. Open tubes of crescent rolls. Roll out dough and pull apart sections. Place the wide end of dough toward the small bowl, continuing around the pan and making sure to overlap each section about $\frac{1}{2}$" and to drape the pointed end over the edge of the pan.

4. Press the bottom of the dough to seal together. Layer with $\frac{1}{2}$ cup cheese, scrambled eggs, $\frac{1}{2}$ cup cheese, bacon, ham, and $\frac{1}{2}$ cup cheese.

5. Fold pointed ends over the filling, tucking inside to seal. Continue with each section, then remove the small bowl.

6. In a separate small bowl, combine butter and garlic salt. Brush top of crescent ring with melted butter and bake for 30 minutes. Remove from oven, sprinkle with remaining $\frac{1}{2}$ cup cheese, and serve.

Izzy's Hawaiian Fruit Salad

My daughter Izzy loves fresh fruit; she is constantly making different fruit side dishes to go with dinner. For this recipe, she added cream cheese and unique fruits, which was genius. This salad is perfect for any meal, or as a side dish for a family picnic or barbecue party. Trust me, this is going to be a keeper, and your family is gonna love it.

Prep Time: 45 minutes
Cook Time: N/A
Yields: 10 servings

Ingredients:

2 (15-ounce) cans mandarin oranges in light syrup, drained
1 whole pineapple, peeled, cored, and cut into chunks
1 (16-ounce) container fresh strawberries, chopped
10 medium kiwis, peeled and cut into chunks
4 medium mangoes, peeled and cut into cubes
2 large papayas, seeded, peeled, and cut into chunks
6 medium bananas, peeled and sliced
3 tablespoons fresh lime juice
2 (8-ounce) blocks cream cheese, softened
2 (5.1-ounce) boxes cheesecake instant pudding mix
2 cups extra creamy vanilla-flavored creamer

Steps:

1. Combine all fruit except bananas in a large bowl.

2. In a small bowl, add sliced bananas and pour lime juice on top and gently stir to coat bananas. Note: This keeps them from turning brown.

3. In a medium bowl, combine cream cheese and pudding mix. Mix with a hand mixer on medium speed until light and fluffy, about 5 minutes. Slowly, add creamer and mix well, about 5–7 minutes.

4. Add bananas to the large fruit bowl and stir gently. Next, fold in the cream mixture carefully until well coated. Refrigerate for 30 minutes and serve.

CHAPTER 4

Fun Pizza-Themed Recipes and Then Some

~ ✳ ~

After becoming foster parents, they adopted Joshua. He overcame many obstacles in his life and learned to make meals with Mom, including pizzas.

When David was two years old, we decided to look into foster care, and that next year we became foster parents. During our first foster parent meeting, I noticed the cutest little boy sitting in the middle of the room playing. He had fire-engine-red hair and the biggest green eyes I had ever seen. Immediately, I fell in love with him, and I knew in my heart that I was meant to be his mother. Right after the meeting, we asked our social worker if he was able to be adopted. She was surprised because we had just become new foster parents and he had some disabilities due to previous injuries. We didn't care; we loved him already and were ready to be his parents.

David loved his new little brother, and there isn't a picture that doesn't have David with his arms wrapped around Joshua, hugging him. Joshua knew that David loved him—you could see it in the way Joshua looked up at David and then smiled the biggest smile. His entire face would light up when he saw his big brother walk into the room, and they were the best friends ever. That next year, on July 2, 2003, his adoption was final, and we were officially parents to two active boys.

Even at a young age, Joshua really loved spending time with me and helping me in the kitchen. I wanted to find a way to create recipes that would be simple to put together so that Joshua could help me with them, and then eventually one day make them by himself. Mini pizzas were my first idea, and we had the best time making dinner for everyone. This turned into a tradition that Joshua and I would do every Friday for pizza night. (We also bought exercise headbands and put them on before we made dinner!) Joshua would giggle the entire time, and he would definitely have the most toppings on his pizza out of everyone else, but that's okay. I loved seeing him so happy and excited to be in the kitchen with me. Now that Joshua is older, I bet you can guess what his favorite meal is: Yep! It's pizza. Because Joshua loved cooking with me and was always asking if we could make pizzas for everyone, I decided that Joshua would be the "official" pizza maker and we now call him the "pizza chef."

When Joshua was little, I had to be careful when cooking because he was sensitive to the texture of certain foods. This of course brought some more challenges when cooking for a family of four. There were times when I had to cook two different styles of dinner, one for my boys and one for me and my husband with more seasonings. I began to slowly introduce different foods to the boys in small amounts with more flavorful dishes. My weekly menu consisted of meals I knew the whole family would eat, but then I'd add a couple new recipes for us all to try out. This was the time that several of the recipes found in this cookbook came to life. Over the years, I have built on those recipes and added different spices or ingredients. But there were several recipes that weren't so successful, and I'd know it was time to order pizza if I saw my husband's and two boys' noses curled up and a look of distress and confusion on their faces!

When we first brought Joshua home and started working with the doctors, they gave us no hope for a "normal" life. It was discouraging because they couldn't answer any of our questions; but now, twenty years later, he cooks dinner by himself, works with Dad on the farm, and got his first job working at the grocery store. He is so successful because we spent years working with him on life skills and not giving up on him. We reassured him that he could do whatever he set his mind to and encouraged him to never give up.

This chapter is perfect for Joshua because he has created some really cool pizza-themed meals that are easy to make and delicious. They are meals that your children can make because the ingredients are simple and the steps are easy to understand. These recipes will bring your whole family together with meals that your kids will love making with you. Sit with your family and pick a day for your themed night. Then let your kiddos choose their own toppings and see what creations they will come up with. Hopefully it will become a family favorite and will start a pizza-themed night with your family. 🌹

Pepperoni Pizza Casserole

When my kids were little, I was always trying to find casserole meals that were kid friendly. My kids loved pasta and pizza, so I thought, "Let's combine the two together." Now Joshua makes this often for our big family and has added new ingredients of his own. This recipe is so easy, has simple ingredients, and takes no time to put together. This is also my go-to meal if I want to make something for a potluck or to help out another family when they are struggling. This recipe is a perfect budget-friendly meal for any family.

Prep Time: 10 minutes
Cook Time: 40 minutes
Yields: 12 servings

Ingredients:

2 (16-ounce) boxes rotini pasta, uncooked

3 (26-ounce) jars spaghetti sauce, any flavor

1 (32-ounce) bag shredded Italian cheese mix

4 (6-ounce) packages sliced pepperoni

2 (5-ounce) packages sliced mini pepperoni

Steps:

1. Preheat oven to 375°F.

2. To a large stockpot of boiling water, add pasta and cook over medium-high heat for 10 minutes or until al dente. Drain pasta and return to pot.

3. Add spaghetti sauce, reserving 1 cup, to the pasta and mix.

4. In 2 ungreased 9" × 13" casserole dishes, spread reserved sauce evenly on the bottom. Next, layer with pasta, cheese, and both types of pepperoni. Repeat layers until casserole dishes are filled. Top with cheese and bake for 30 minutes. Serve.

Joshua's Italian Salad

This salad goes great with any Italian-themed dinner. Joshua also makes this quite a bit in the summertime to pair with burgers or brats off the grill. This recipe is super easy and keeps in the fridge for days—if it lasts that long. You can also make your own salad dressing simply by combining olive oil, red wine vinegar, salt, black pepper, and dried Italian seasoning. Shake and go! Or make it ahead of time and keep it in the fridge, then use as needed.

Prep Time: 20 minutes
Cook Time: N/A
Yields: 10 servings

Ingredients:

2 (16-ounce) boxes rotini pasta, cooked according to package directions, drained, and cooled

3 cups peeled and cubed cucumbers

3 cups cherry tomatoes, cut into halves

3 cups cubed salami

2 (8-ounce) packages block medium Cheddar cheese, cut into 1" cubes

2 (8-ounce) packages block Monterey jack cheese, cut into 1" cubes

2 (9.5-ounce) jars pitted kalamata olives, drained and kept whole

1 (21-ounce) jar pitted green olives, drained and kept whole

1 (24-ounce) bottle zesty Italian salad dressing

Steps:

1. In a large bowl, combine all ingredients except dressing. With a large spoon, fold ingredients together.

2. Add dressing and stir again. Store in the fridge until ready to serve.

Italian Sub Sliders

Whenever we go out for lunch, my husband and boys order Italian subs. So of course, I wanted to try to create that sub sandwich at home but with slider rolls—and make enough to feed our entire family. It makes for a great lunch idea, especially when we are busy haying in the summer, because I can cut them into sections, wrap them up, and haul them to the farm workers to serve with chips and nice cold water.

Prep Time: 35 minutes
Cook Time: 35 minutes
Yields: 12 servings

Ingredients:

2 (24-count) packages Hawaiian sweet rolls

2 cups mayonnaise

2 (24-count) packages sliced Colby cheese

2 (16-ounce) containers sliced honey ham

$\frac{1}{2}$ cup yellow mustard

1 (16-ounce) package bacon, cooked and chopped

4 (11-count) packages sliced Havarti cheese

2 (16-ounce) containers sliced roast beef

2 (24-count) packages sliced medium Cheddar cheese

1 cup banana pepper rings, drained

2 (16-ounce) packages sliced smoked turkey

2 (24-count) packages sliced Swiss cheese

$\frac{1}{2}$ cup Dijon mustard

4 (8-ounce) packages sliced salami

4 cups shredded medium Cheddar cheese

1 (24-ounce) bottle Italian dressing

Steps:

1. Preheat oven to 350°F.

2. Place rolls on 2 ungreased 18" × 26" baking sheets. Slice each loaf of rolls horizontally and layer the inside of tops and bottoms with mayo. Bake for 15 minutes, then remove and let stand for 10 minutes.

3. Layer bottoms with ingredients in order listed, reserving the dressing. Place tops on rolls and brush with Italian dressing. Bake for another 20 minutes. Serve.

Noah's Homemade Hot Pockets

We are always looking for new ways to create different and cool pizza recipes. I love that my eight kids are comfortable in the kitchen. They come up to me asking if I can help them get the ingredients to make dinner. Noah is my grab-and-go type of guy, and he wanted to make his own pizza pockets. They turned out great!

Prep Time: 25 minutes
Cook Time: 30 minutes
Yields: 12 servings

Ingredients:

2 (2-count) packages premade pizza crust

6 cups shredded mozzarella cheese

2 (24-ounce) jars spaghetti sauce, any flavor

10 tablespoons dried Italian seasoning, divided

2 (8-ounce) packages sliced salami

4 (1.5-ounce) packages sliced pepperoni

3 pounds ground pork sausage, cooked

½ cup salted butter, melted

Steps:

1. Preheat oven to 375°F.

2. Remove 4 crusts from packages and roll out 2 crusts together on a floured surface. Repeat with 2 remaining crusts. Carefully place each prepared crust on its own greased 18" × 26" baking sheet.

3. In the center of each crust, layer cheese, sauce, 1 tablespoon seasoning, salami, cheese, pepperoni, cheese, sauce, sausage, cheese, sauce, and 1 tablespoon seasoning. Leave a few inches around all four sides for folding. Be sure to reserve a bit of cheese for later.

4. Fold the top and bottom in toward the filling, then fold over the sides to encase the filling, overlapping them and pinching them together to seal the dough.

5. Brush tops with melted butter and sprinkle each with ½ tablespoon seasoning.

6. Bake for 30 minutes and then remove from oven and sprinkle with reserved cheese (the heat from the hot pocket will melt the cheese). Serve with warm spaghetti sauce for dipping.

Cast Iron Italian Sub Ring

Using my cast iron pan is my favorite way to cook. There are so many different pans and bakeware, but this is my favorite. Making a ring is another way to make the perfect lunch or dinner. It's a wonderful substitute for sandwiches, and you can place a bowl inside and fill it with ranch dressing for dipping.

Prep Time: 30 minutes
Cook Time: 35 minutes
Yields: 10 servings

Ingredients:

4 (8-ounce) tubes sweet Hawaiian crescent rolls

1 (16-ounce) package sliced pepper jack cheese

2 (8-ounce) packages sliced salami

1 (16-ounce) package sliced provolone cheese

8 tablespoons Dijon mustard

2 (8-ounce) packages sliced pepperoni

2 (8-ounce) packages sliced mozzarella cheese

1 cup Italian dressing, divided

1 cup banana pepper rings, drained

2 (8-ounce) packages sliced pastrami

1 (16-ounce) package sliced medium Cheddar cheese

4 tablespoons dried oregano, divided

Steps:

1. Preheat oven to 375°F.

2. In the middle of a 17" round cast iron pan, place a small (3") bowl upside down. Open 2 tubes of crescent rolls. Roll out dough and pull apart sections. Place the triangles of dough in a ring around the pan, with the wide ends near the bowl in the center. Continue around the pan, making sure to overlap each section about ½" and drape the pointed end over the outer edge of the pan.

3. Repeat with the remaining 2 tubes crescent rolls and another cast iron pan.

4. Press the bottom of the dough to seal together. Remove bowl and divide ingredients into two equal portions. Layer the ingredients in the following order: pepper jack cheese, salami, provolone, mustard, pepperoni, mozzarella, ½ cup Italian dressing, banana peppers, pastrami, and Cheddar. Sprinkle each sub ring with 1 tablespoon oregano.

5. After you have added all the ingredients, fold pointed ends of crescent rolls over the filling, tucking inside to seal. Brush with remaining ½ cup Italian dressing and sprinkle with remaining oregano.

6. Bake for 35 minutes or until top has browned. Serve.

Stuffed Pizza Pies

Normally, we like to make pizza calzones or pasty pies, but this is great if you're in a hurry. You just layer the ingredients and done! We are always looking for different easy-to-make pizza recipes. Joshua is super great at creating new ones just like this one for our big family. It really is nice when my kids decide to make dinner and I get a night or two off, plus they make the best meals. I just sit at the counter and watch them. It makes my heart happy.

Prep Time: 20 minutes
Cook Time: 50 minutes
Yields: 10 servings

Ingredients:

4 (2-count) boxes refrigerated premade store-bought pizza or pie crusts

1 (29-ounce) can tomato sauce

4 tablespoons dried Italian seasoning

8 cups shredded mozzarella cheese

2 (8-ounce) packages large, thin-sliced pepperoni

2 (5-ounce) packages sliced mini pepperoni

4 cups shredded Parmesan cheese

2 (8-ounce) packages sliced large salami

1 (8-ounce) jar sun-dried tomatoes, drained and chopped

8 large egg whites, slightly beaten

Steps:

1. Preheat oven to 375°F.

2. Grab four round 9" glass pie plates. Roll out all 8 crusts and place 4 in the bottom of each pie plate. Poke holes using a fork and bake for 10 minutes, then remove and let stand.

3. Layer bottom of each baked crust with some sauce, seasoning, 1 cup mozzarella, pepperoni slices, mini pepperoni, ½ cup Parmesan, salami, and sun-dried tomatoes. Repeat the layers, then end with more sauce and seasoning. Top with another crust and seal edges with a fork. Cut about 6 (1") air holes and brush with egg whites.

4. Bake for 40 minutes. Serve.

Homemade Hawaiian Pizzas

Hawaiian pizza is my and my son Gideon's favorite pizza of all time, and when we add bacon to it, it makes it even better. Our family likes to make pizzas for special holidays and on weekends. Sometimes we will make these as mini pizzas so we can all make our pizza just how we like it. We actually eat a lot of pizza because it's so easy to make and super-fast to eat.

Prep Time: 20 minutes
Cook Time: 25 minutes
Yields: 10 servings

Ingredients:

3 (2-count) packages premade pizza crust

2 (14-ounce) jars pizza sauce

4 tablespoons dried Italian seasoning

2 (16-ounce) packages bacon, cooked and chopped

6 cups chopped pineapple (fresh or canned), drained

1 (16-ounce) package deli smoked ham, chopped

2 (3-ounce) packages prosciutto, chopped

2 medium red onions, peeled and sliced thin

8 cups shredded mozzarella cheese

Steps:

1. Preheat oven to 375°F.

2. Roll out each pizza crust into a rectangular shape and place 3 crusts together on ungreased 18" × 26" baking sheets. Make sure to overlap and pinch edges for a continuous crust.

3. Layer crusts with pizza sauce and sprinkle 2 tablespoons Italian seasoning per pizza. Layer remaining ingredients and top each pizza with 4 cups cheese.

4. Bake for 25 minutes. Serve.

Pepperoni Pizza Monkey Bread

My family loves the traditional cinnamon monkey bread, and I was looking for something fun to make for lunch for my eight kids. Well, we love pizza, and I thought it was the perfect idea! I was so excited that it stayed together after I baked it and flipped it over. My kids were impressed, and we had a hard time eating it because it looked so beautiful. The kids made a garlic butter pizza sauce to dip it into, and it's the perfect touch!

Prep Time: 30 minutes
Cook Time: 40 minutes
Yields: 10 servings

Ingredients:

1 cup salted butter, softened

1 tablespoon minced fresh garlic

2 tablespoons finely chopped fresh parsley

$\frac{1}{2}$ teaspoon salt

$\frac{1}{2}$ teaspoon ground black pepper

1 teaspoon dried basil

$\frac{1}{2}$ teaspoon dried thyme

2 (8-count) cans original Grands! Biscuits

2 (5-ounce) packages sliced mini pepperoni

2 (8-ounce) bags shredded Italian cheese mix

$\frac{1}{2}$ cup salted butter, melted

1 (14-ounce) jar pizza sauce

2 teaspoons garlic powder

Steps:

1. Preheat oven to 375°F.

2. In a medium bowl, combine 1 cup softened butter, garlic, parsley, salt, pepper, basil, and thyme and mix until smooth. Lightly brush some of butter mixture on the inside of an 11" Bundt pan.

3. Tear each biscuit into four parts and roll them into balls. Place some in a single layer on bottom of pan and brush with more butter mixture. Next, layer with mini pepperoni and cheese.

4. Repeat layers until you have reached the top of the pan, making sure to end with biscuits, then spread a layer of butter mixture to finish.

5. Bake for 40 minutes or until biscuits are cooked through. Once cooked, remove from oven and let stand 15 minutes, then flip onto a serving tray and brush on more butter mixture and sprinkle with remaining cheese.

6. In a small bowl, combine $\frac{1}{2}$ cup melted butter with 1 cup pizza sauce and garlic powder. Place bowl inside the baked monkey bread ring.

7. To eat, pull apart bread and dip into prepared dip.

Joshua's Meat Trio–Filled Rolls

When my boys were playing football and it was our turn to make dinner before the game, I decided to use Joshua's recipe for pizza rolls but make it bigger and played with the fillings because this was one hungry crew. These were so simple to make and had so much filling inside that I doubled the recipe and made four rolls that literally fed the entire football team. They were a hit and not one crumb was left.

Prep Time: 30 minutes
Cook Time: 50 minutes
Yields: 12 servings

Ingredients:

2 pounds 90/10 lean ground beef

2 tablespoons minced fresh garlic

2 tablespoons dried Italian seasoning

2 tablespoons dried minced onion

2 (2-count) packages premade pizza crusts

2 (14-ounce) jars pizza sauce

2 pounds ground Italian sausage, cooked and drained

2 (16-ounce) packages bacon, cooked and chopped

6 cups shredded fiesta blend cheese mix

Steps:

1. Preheat oven to 375°F.

2. In a large saucepan, combine beef, garlic, Italian seasoning, and minced onion. Cook over medium heat for 15 minutes or until cooked through, stirring occasionally. Drain liquid and set meat aside.

3. On a floured 18" × 26" baking sheet, place 2 pizza crusts beside each other and press together, forming a rectangle in the middle of the pan. Repeat with the other 2 crusts on another sheet.

4. Layer crusts with pizza sauce, beef, sausage, bacon, and cheese, reserving about 1 cup of cheese for later use. Leave a few inches around all four sides for folding. Repeat layers if you want them extra stuffed. Pull the top and bottom ends over filling and then fold over the sides to encase filling. Make sure to pinch dough together at the top to seal.

5. Bake for 35 minutes. Remove from oven and sprinkle with reserved cheese. Let stand 15 minutes to allow filling to set up. Serve.

Pizza Sliders

There hasn't been a meal I haven't turned into a full dinner with slider rolls. What I like about using sliders is the sweetness of the bread goes great with salty, savory, and sweet flavors. Honestly, I kinda became a little obsessed with challenging myself to come up with new recipes using them. They are great to use when you are pressed for time and have to just grab items out of the fridge to make a fast meal. Spread the rolls with butter and top with your favorite pizza toppings, then bake and serve. It's that easy.

Prep Time: 30 minutes
Cook Time: 35 minutes
Yields: 10 servings

Ingredients:

2 (24-count) packages Hawaiian sweet rolls

2 cups salted butter, melted, divided

2 teaspoons garlic powder

2 teaspoons onion powder

2 (14-ounce) jars pizza sauce

2 (8-ounce) packages sliced mozzarella cheese

2 (8-ounce) packages sliced pepperoni

2 (8-ounce) packages sliced provolone cheese

4 (5-ounce) packages shredded Parmesan cheese

2 tablespoons dried oregano

1 tablespoon dried basil

1/2 teaspoon crushed red pepper flakes

Steps:

1. Preheat oven to 375°F.

2. Cut rolls in half horizontally and place tops and bottoms on separate, ungreased 18" × 26" baking sheets. Brush both with 1 cup melted butter, then sprinkle with garlic powder and onion powder. Bake for 15 minutes.

3. Layer bottoms with pizza sauce, mozzarella, pepperoni, provolone, more pepperoni, Parmesan, and more sauce. Place tops on.

4. In a small bowl, combine remaining 1 cup melted butter, oregano, basil, and red pepper flakes. Whisk and brush over the tops of the rolls.

5. Bake for 20 minutes. Serve.

Grinder Sliders

These sliders are amazing. When I made them, my son Gideon walked up to me and hugged me, then looked at me and said, "These are the best sliders you have ever made!" When I ask my kids what they want me to make for dinner or lunch, Gideon now requests these Grinder Sliders every time. What is nice is that you can cook the meats first, then add the fresh veggies to the slider right before you serve it.

Prep Time: 30 minutes
Cook Time: 20 minutes
Yields: 10 servings

Ingredients:

2 (24-count) packages Hawaiian sweet rolls

1 cup mayonnaise

2 (8-ounce) packages sliced Havarti cheese

1 (16-ounce) package sliced deli turkey

1 (16-ounce) package sliced Colby jack cheese

1 (16-ounce) package sliced deli smoked ham

1 (16-ounce) package sliced provolone cheese

1 head iceberg lettuce, chopped

6 medium tomatoes, sliced thin

1 (16-ounce) jar banana pepper rings, drained

2 teaspoons salt

2 teaspoons ground black pepper

6 tablespoons red wine vinegar

1 cup avocado oil (or olive oil)

1 cup yellow mustard

1 cup Dijon mustard

Steps:

1. Preheat oven to 375°F.

2. Cut rolls in half horizontally and place the bottoms on ungreased 18" × 26" baking sheets. Spread mayo on bottom of rolls, then layer Havarti, half of the turkey, Colby jack, half of the ham, provolone, and remaining ham and turkey. Bake for 15 minutes.

3. Remove from oven and top with lettuce, tomatoes, and banana peppers.

4. In a small bowl, combine salt, black pepper, vinegar, and oil. Drizzle mixture over sliders.

5. Brush both mustards on the inside of top rolls, then place on top and serve.

CHAPTER 5

Land and Sea Recipes

~✳~

After the Bells tried for eight long years to have a baby, Gideon was born. He loves to fish and spend time outdoors.

When I was twenty-one years old, I was diagnosed with an aggressive form of endometriosis. After the doctor told me the diagnosis, I was confused because I had no idea what it meant. The next sentence from the doctor was to inform me that the chances of me being able to have a child naturally were slim or next to impossible. I was heartbroken, and it took me many tears to see that our infertility journey was a way for God to provide us other opportunities, like adopting our first son David, then Joshua through foster care, plus the opportunity to help dozens of other children that came in and out of our home throughout our ten-plus years as foster parents.

Well, after eight long years, and exactly one day after Joshua's adoption was final, I found out I was pregnant with Gideon. We called my husband and David told him, "Mommy has a baby in her belly." We were so excited that God had answered our prayers, and Gideon was born the next year. He looked just like Luke, and as he got older, I could tell that he was interested in the same things as his dad. He wanted to go fishing and hunting, he enjoyed walking in the woods, and he loved working on the farm. Gideon would grab a chair and take it outside to watch Dad cook dinner on the grill, then run back inside and open the fridge to grab two pops. They would sit by the grill, looking at the woods, while drinking pop and waiting for the burgers to be done.

I knew that he would walk in his dad's footsteps in enjoying the outdoors and trying his hand at the grill. Now that he is older, the two of them are constantly in competition on who can cook the better steak or burger on the grill, and they are always giving each other "cooking tips" to "help" the other grill better foods.

After Gideon was born, I began to realize that having three growing boys meant that my once-a-month grocery hauls would turn into weekly grocery hauls. My husband had to build a pantry in my laundry room to hold more snacks, canned goods, and our weekly meal items. Just to be safe we also bought an extra freezer to store meats and chicken that I would find on sale so we could stock up. I was nervous at the thought of cooking for my hardworking husband and now three very busy boys that love to snack all day, every day. So not only was I having to come up with three hearty meals a day but now I was also trying to come up with snack ideas for in between meals. I felt like my boys were hungry *all the time*, and a couple of crackers here and there weren't working anymore. As the boys grew, they wanted to go grocery shopping with me, but then I felt like we'd buy more than I'd planned on. Once we got home and started to unpack the groceries, I would find snack cakes that I didn't remember even putting into my cart, as the boys giggled in the other room.

The boys also all wanted to start helping me even more in the kitchen when I made breakfast, lunch, and dinner. Gideon would ask to be in charge of grilling the hot dogs for our beanie weenies or to add to my homemade mac and cheese. Needless to say, we ate *a lot* of hot dogs when the boys were younger because I didn't have the heart to tell him we didn't need the grill for every meal—so I spent the extra money to buy all beef hot dogs and made sure to buy sides that worked perfectly with hot dogs. I think that Gideon wanted to show Dad that he could cook on the grill like a big boy, making sure to grab his chair and pop while he cooked dinner for us. Gideon knew that Dad worked hard for us every single day, and this way he could relax when he got home.

With Gideon's fishing skills leading to more fresh fish in the house, I started to create many of the recipes in this chapter. When he was old enough, he bought his very own boat to go fishing. At the end of each day of fishing he would proudly walk into the kitchen with his catch to help with dinner. There isn't a day that goes by where I don't open my freezers at the barn and find dozens of trout, white fish, salmon, or perch in there.

Each of our children gets to choose a senior trip before they graduate high school. When we gave Gideon a choice to go anywhere, he said he had always wanted to go to Florida to fish off the beach on the Atlantic Ocean. I have never seen him smile so much, standing on the beach with his bare feet and a fishing pole in his hand. I will always remember his reaction when he caught the biggest fish I had ever seen. Before we came home, we packed all the fish into a cooler and brought them home on the plane. That night, Gideon made the best grilled fish dinner for our family with perfect spices plus fresh garden veggies on the side.

Gideon is such a natural when it comes to pairing spices that make his fresh-caught fish even better, like lemon pepper seasoning or cayenne pepper and fresh minced garlic. No matter what he chooses, it always tastes great paired with my Homemade Tartar Sauce (see recipe in this chapter), which he asks me to make every time he serves fish for dinner! Here are land and sea recipes inspired by Gideon's fresh-caught fish. 🌹

Gideon's Cajun Shrimp Boil

My son Gideon is the fisherman of the family. Every day I look out the window and see him pulling his boat out to the lake. He loves all kinds of seafood and asked if he could make our family a shrimp boil for our big Saturday dinner. So, we headed to the grocery store and got everything he had on his list. Gideon came home and grabbed the biggest stockpot I had and began to make magic. You can serve this over rice if desired.

Prep Time: 35 minutes
Cook Time: 35 minutes
Yields: 12–14 servings

Ingredients:

1 (89-ounce) jug orange juice

1 (16-ounce) bottle lemon juice

1 (4.25-ounce) bottle lemon pepper seasoning

4 tablespoons cayenne pepper

6 tablespoons Old Bay Seasoning

1 (4.25-ounce) bottle paprika

2 (4.25-ounce) bottles garlic powder

2 (4.25-ounce) bottles onion powder

2 (13.5-ounce) packages andouille sausage, sliced

2 large red onions, peeled and sliced

1 (5-pound) bag small red potatoes

12 large ears corn, shucked and cut into halves

2 (2-pound) bags frozen, raw, peeled, and deveined large shrimp, tails off

2 (1-pound) bags frozen jumbo sea scallops

Steps:

1. Combine orange juice, lemon juice, lemon pepper seasoning, cayenne pepper, Old Bay Seasoning, paprika, garlic powder, and onion powder in a large stockpot. (Depending on how spicy you want your boil, adjust the seasonings according to taste.)

2. Add sausage, onions, potatoes, and corn to the pot and then cook over medium-low heat for 20 minutes or until veggies are soft, stirring occasionally.

3. Reduce heat to low and add seafood. Simmer for an additional 15 minutes, stirring as needed.

4. Let stand for 10 minutes, then remove sausage, veggies, and seafood from stock and let rest another 20 minutes before serving.

Izzy's Salmon *and* Cream Cheese Sushi Rolls

Our family, believe it or not, really likes sushi. We often head to our local sushi restaurant for lunch. Izzy was determined to figure out how to make sushi at home to help save us money. She ordered all the cooking utensils she would need all by herself. Since then, she makes sushi for us all the time and adds different ingredients into it to try out on us. These salmon sushi rolls are amazing. She's even used salmon that we caught while in Alaska on vacation. They turn out so yummy every time. Make sure to have a bowl of ice water on hand to keep your seaweed from sticking when constructing rolls.

Prep Time: 30 minutes
Cook Time: 20 minutes
Yields: 10 servings

Sushi Rice Ingredients:

6 cups water

5 cups sushi rice

2 tablespoons white rice

1 teaspoon white sugar

1 teaspoon Himalayan salt

1/2 cup rice vinegar

Sushi Roll Ingredients:

3 (10-count) packages sushi nori sheets

4 large ripe avocados, pitted, peeled, and sliced thin

4 medium cucumbers, peeled and sliced thin lengthwise

2 (10-ounce) bags matchstick carrots

2 (8-ounce) blocks cream cheese, softened and sliced into thin strips

3 (6-ounce) raw salmon filets, sliced thin

Dipping Sauce Ingredients:

1/2 cup rice vinegar

1/2 cup soy sauce

2 teaspoons sesame oil

2 teaspoons crushed red pepper flakes

Steps:

1. **Make the Sushi Rice:** In a medium saucepan, combine water and both kinds of rice. Bring to a boil over high heat, and once it is boiling, cook for an additional 3 minutes. Turn down heat to low and simmer for 15 minutes with lid on.

2. Grease an 18" × 26" baking sheet and add rice to the sheet, pressing it down evenly. Sprinkle rice with sugar, salt, and vinegar. Using a spatula, flip rice over and continue flipping until rice becomes room temperature. Set aside.

3. **Make the Sushi Rolls:** Lay down a sheet of nori. Place about 1/2 cup rice 3/4" away from edges, making sure to press down to flatten. Layer rice with veggies, cream cheese, and salmon. Roll seaweed up with your thumbs, making sure your fingers are inside pressing down on the ingredients and tucking them. When you get 1/2" away from the end, wet the ends with water and seal the roll. Carefully, cut sushi into 3/4" sections. Repeat with remaining nori.

4. **Make the Dipping Sauce:** In a small bowl, combine all Dipping Sauce ingredients and serve alongside the Sushi Rolls.

Gideon's Chicken Wings— 3 Ways

One of Gideon's favorite things to make for our weekend football-watching parties is chicken wings. He is always messaging me asking to add wings to my grocery list. He has come up with some pretty inventive flavors. Wings are great for a big family because you can buy them in bulk, season, bake, and serve. Our number one dipping choice for these wings is ranch dressing. These wings also go great served with French fries.

Prep Time: 30 minutes
Cook Time: 1 hour
Yields: 12–14 servings

Additional Ingredients:
3 (4-pound) bags frozen, all natural chicken wings

Marinade Ingredients:
1 (33-ounce) bottle avocado oil (or olive oil)
2 tablespoons salt
1 tablespoon ground black pepper

Ranch Seasoning Ingredients:
4 (1-ounce) packets dry ranch seasoning mix
$\frac{1}{2}$ teaspoon paprika
$\frac{1}{2}$ teaspoon garlic powder
$\frac{1}{2}$ teaspoon onion powder

Buffalo Seasoning Ingredients:
$\frac{1}{2}$ cup Frank's RedHot Original Cayenne Pepper Sauce
$\frac{1}{2}$ cup salted butter, melted
1 tablespoon garlic powder
1 tablespoon white vinegar

Honey Mustard Ingredients:
$\frac{1}{2}$ cup honey
$\frac{1}{2}$ cup Dijon mustard
$\frac{1}{4}$ cup mayonnaise
1 tablespoon salt
$\frac{1}{2}$ tablespoon ground black pepper
1 tablespoon dried parsley

Steps:

1. Preheat oven to 375°F.

2. **Make the Marinade:** In a large bowl, combine all Marinade ingredients and whisk together. Coat each wing in Marinade and place onto 3 ungreased 18" × 26" baking sheets. Bake for 45 minutes.

3. **Make the Sauces:** In three separate medium bowls, combine each of the three different sauce ingredients and mix well.

4. Remove wings from oven and increase heat to 400°F.

5. Coat each pan of wings with one of the three sauces.

6. Cook wings until internal temperature reaches 165°F, about 30 minutes, then remove from oven and let stand for 10 minutes. Serve with your choice of dipping sauce.

Creamy Shrimp *and* Grits

I was raised in the South and absolutely love cheesy grits with lots of butter, salt, and pepper. My family just doesn't understand my love for grits because they are all "Northerners." When I traveled to Florida to visit my sisters, I had the best shrimp and grits, and I knew that I had to try my hand at making it at home for my family. The best part of the meal was how creamy and smooth it turned out. So yummy! Now, finally, I think most of my family understands my love for grits.

Prep Time: 30 minutes

Cook Time: 1 hour and **5** minutes

Yields: 12 servings

Grits Ingredients:

4 cups water

4 cups chicken broth

2 cups grits

1 teaspoon cayenne pepper

1 teaspoon ground black pepper

2 teaspoons salt

2 cups shredded medium Cheddar cheese

2 cups shredded Italian cheese mix

$\frac{1}{2}$ cup salted butter

Shrimp Mixture Ingredients:

1 (16-ounce) package bacon, cut into pieces

1 large yellow onion, peeled and chopped

1 tablespoon garlic powder

1 tablespoon dried parsley

2 (2-pound) bags frozen, raw, peeled, and deveined large shrimp, tails off

1 tablespoon minced fresh garlic

$\frac{1}{2}$ cup chicken broth

Roux Ingredients:

$\frac{1}{2}$ cup salted butter

1 cup all-purpose flour

$\frac{1}{2}$ tablespoon paprika

1 teaspoon salt

1 teaspoon ground black pepper

2 cups heavy cream

2 cups sauce from Shrimp Mixture

1 (8-ounce) container mascarpone cheese

2 cups whole milk

Steps:

1. **Make the Grits:** In a large stockpot, combine water, 4 cups broth, grits, both peppers, and salt and cook over medium-low heat for 25 minutes, stirring occasionally.

2. Once grits are creamy and smooth, remove from heat and add both shredded cheeses and butter. Stir to melt cheese, place lid on pot, and set aside.

continued

continued

3. **Make the Shrimp Mixture:** In a large saucepan, add chopped bacon and cook over medium heat for 5 minutes. Then add onion and continue to cook for another 5 minutes.

4. Add garlic powder, parsley, shrimp, minced garlic, and ½ cup broth. Reduce heat to low and simmer for 10 minutes, stirring occasionally.

5. Ladle out approximately 2 cups of the resulting sauce and set aside.

6. **Make the Roux:** To another large saucepan, add butter, flour, paprika, salt, and pepper. Whisk over medium heat until a paste forms, about 2 minutes, and then let simmer for 3 minutes. Slowly, whisk in cream, then the reserved sauce from the Shrimp Mixture.

7. Stir in mascarpone. Slowly, whisk in milk over medium heat until cream thickens, about 5 minutes. Using a slotted spoon, remove Shrimp Mixture from pan and add to pan with the cream sauce. Stir together and serve over cheesy Grits.

Shrimp, Scallops, *and* Lobster Scampi

Our family really likes seafood; in fact, we eat at our local seafood restaurant every couple of weeks. One of our favorite dishes is scampi. When my husband and I went to Alaska for our ten-year anniversary, the seafood dishes were so amazing and they had capers in every meal. The capers added the perfect salty taste to the dishes. I came home and right away bought capers and added it to whatever dish I could. They go really well with this Shrimp, Scallops, and Lobster Scampi, and for an additional flavor I added in some sun-dried tomatoes.

Prep Time: 40 minutes
Cook Time: 30 minutes
Yields: 10–12 servings

Ingredients:

½ cup salted butter

¼ cup avocado oil (or olive oil)

2 tablespoons minced fresh garlic

1 teaspoon crushed red pepper flakes

1 tablespoon garlic salt

2 (7-ounce) packages lobster tails (about 2 tails)

4 pounds frozen, raw, peeled, and deveined medium shrimp, tails on

2 (16-ounce) bags frozen scallops

4 tablespoons lemon juice

⅔ cup white cooking wine

2 (3.5-ounce) jars capers, drained

2 (8.5-ounce) jars sun-dried tomatoes, drained and chopped

2 (16-ounce) boxes linguine pasta, cooked al dente

1 bunch fresh parsley, chopped

3 cups shredded Parmesan cheese

Steps:

1. In a large saucepan, combine butter, oil, minced garlic, red pepper flakes, and garlic salt. Cook over medium heat for 5 minutes, stirring occasionally.

2. Remove meat from lobster tails and cut into 1" chunks. Add shrimp, scallops, and lobster to saucepan and continue to cook for 15 minutes, stirring occasionally, or until the seafood is opaque on both sides.

3. Reduce heat to low. Add lemon juice, wine, capers, and sun-dried tomatoes. Simmer for 10 minutes stirring occasionally.

4. Add linguine and mix well. Serve garnished with parsley and cheese.

Izzy's Teriyaki Chicken Pineapple Bowls

Izabella really likes to make meals that are unique and to present them like a professional chef. She notices the little things and adds small details to make her meals fancy, like adding fresh herbs as a garnish and plating the dish as if you were eating at a 4-star restaurant. I love when she walks into the kitchen and you can see in her face that she is thinking of making something simple yet elegant. This recipe is a perfect example of her style of cooking. It's all about the presentation.

Prep Time: 35 minutes
Cook Time: 50 minutes
Yields: 10 servings

Ingredients:

5 whole pineapples
5 cups uncooked jasmine rice
7 1/2 cups water
4 tablespoons olive oil
5 pounds boneless, skinless chicken breasts, cut into 1/2" cubes
1 teaspoon garlic salt
1 teaspoon white ground pepper
5 tablespoons packed light brown sugar
2 tablespoons minced fresh garlic
4 tablespoons fresh pineapple juice
3 teaspoons diced fresh gingerroot
1 tablespoon honey
2 teaspoons sesame oil
2/3 cup soy sauce
2 tablespoons sesame seeds
1 bunch green onions, ends trimmed, sliced thin

Steps:

1. Prepare pineapples by cutting them into two equal halves, removing cores, and then cutting the center fruit out, preserving the shells. Reserve juices and dice fruit middles into small pieces. Set aside.

2. In a large stockpot, combine rice and water and cook over high heat. Once the whole surface is rippling, edges are bubbling, and white foam forms, reduce heat to low, put lid on pot, and cook for 12 minutes. Remove from heat and let stand for 10 minutes; do not lift the lid. Fluff with a fork before serving.

3. Heat oil in a large skillet over medium heat. Add chicken, garlic salt, and pepper and sauté for 10 minutes, stirring occasionally, then add sugar, garlic, pineapple juice, gingerroot, honey, sesame oil, and soy sauce. Reduce heat to low and simmer for 10 minutes, making sure to stir often. Add diced pineapple, then simmer for another 10 minutes.

4. Fill half of each pineapple with a scoop of rice topped with a scoop of the chicken. Sprinkle with sesame seeds and green onions. If you have any sauce leftover, drizzle over top. Serve.

Grilled Dill Salmon *with* Homemade Tartar Sauce

We took our boys to Alaska for my husband's fiftieth birthday so we could take him salmon fishing. We had a blast and caught over one hundred pounds of salmon. The boys were so excited to bring the fish home and make a family meal for us all. Fish is so easy to cook and good for you. Throwing it on a grill like in this recipe is the best way to cook fish, but it also tastes wonderful baked in the oven.

Prep Time: 30 minutes
Cook Time: 25 minutes
Yields: 10 servings

Tartar Sauce Ingredients:

2 cups mayonnaise

2 tablespoons Dijon mustard

2 tablespoons zucchini sweet relish or regular sweet relish

Salmon Ingredients:

3 pounds fresh salmon filets

1 cup salted butter, sliced

1 tablespoon garlic powder

1 tablespoon onion powder

1 cup diced fresh dill

4 medium lemons, cut into halves

Steps:

1. Preheat grill for 15 minutes to at least 350°F.

2. **Make the Tartar Sauce:** In a medium bowl, combine all Tartar Sauce ingredients and mix well. Store in fridge until Salmon is ready to serve.

3. **Make the Salmon:** On a grill-safe, greased 18" × 26" baking sheet, add salmon (skin side down), butter slices, garlic, onion, and dill. Grill for 15 minutes, then squeeze lemon over all filets. Grill with the lid closed for another 10 minutes or until salmon is flaky.

4. Remove from grill and serve with Homemade Tartar Sauce.

Noah's Venison Stir-Fry

Since I have six boys in the house who like to hunt, my freezer is full of wild game. What's even better is that they are also quite the chefs when it comes to making dinner for us. They know exactly what spices to use to make the meat taste delicious. Noah did a great job on this stir-fry. He wouldn't even let me give him any tips; this was a dinner he wanted to make all by himself. To garnish, you can drizzle with additional soy sauce if desired.

Prep Time: 30 minutes
Cook Time: 40 minutes
Yields: 10 servings

Ingredients:
1/2 cup salted butter
2 tablespoons minced fresh garlic
1 large yellow onion, peeled and diced
1 medium red bell pepper, seeded and diced
5 cups uncooked instant white rice
5 cups water
12 large whole portobello mushrooms, diced
5 pounds lean venison steak, cut into 1" cubes
1 tablespoon garlic powder
1 tablespoon onion powder
1 teaspoon paprika
1/2 cup soy sauce

Steps:

1. In a large saucepan over medium heat, add butter, minced garlic, diced onion, and pepper and sauté for 15 minutes, stirring often.

2. While veggies are cooking, in a separate saucepan combine rice and water and cook over medium heat for 10 minutes or until rice is tender. Remove from heat, place the lid on top, and let stand for 10 minutes.

3. To the pan with veggies, add mushrooms, venison, garlic powder, onion powder, paprika, and soy sauce. Continue cooking over medium heat, stirring occasionally, for 15 minutes, making sure venison is completely cooked through.

4. Serve venison and veggies over rice.

Maple *and* Pepper Bacon Pork Chops

Our family loves bacon, and I try to add it to whatever recipes I can. We tap our maple trees each spring and boil the sap down and use it for baking and dinner recipes. It makes my pepper maple bacon taste amazing. This recipe is so easy to make and adds so much flavor to the chops. Try pairing these chops with rice, mashed potatoes, or air-fried potato wedges drizzled with the drippings from the pepper bacon glaze.

Prep Time: 25 minutes
Cook Time: 45 minutes
Yields: 10 servings

Ingredients:

2 (16-ounce) packages bacon, chopped

2 tablespoons salted butter

1 large yellow onion, peeled and chopped

1 cup peeled and chopped shallots

$1/2$ cup pure maple syrup

1 tablespoon Dijon mustard

$1/4$ cup packed light brown sugar

2 teaspoons ground black pepper

2 teaspoons garlic salt

10 (6-ounce) pork chops

Steps:

1. In a large skillet over medium heat, add bacon and cook for 10 minutes. Add butter, onions, and shallots and continue cooking, stirring occasionally, for 10 minutes or until the veggies are transparent.

2. Add maple syrup, mustard, sugar, pepper, and garlic salt. Turn heat down to low and simmer for 10 minutes, stirring often.

3. Add pork chops to pan, raise heat to medium, and cook for 6 minutes. Then flip over chops and cook another 6 minutes or until chops are cooked through. Serve chops over starch of your choice and top with maple pepper bacon mixture.

U.P. Cudighi Sausage Burgers

When we tell people we live in the Upper Peninsula, they either ask if that's in the United States or they look at us with a confused look. If you're wondering, it's the upper peninsula of Michigan. If you live above the Mackinac Bridge, you are a "Yooper," and if you live below the bridge, you're a "Troll." We live in a Finnish community, and cudighi is a very popular dish up here. Cudighi has a sweet and spicy flavor to it because of the pepper and pumpkin-type spices added to it. Serve these burgers with fries or Homemade Potato Salad.

Prep Time: 25 minutes
Cook Time: 10 minutes
Yields: 12 servings

Ingredients:

6 pounds ground pork

1½ cups red cooking wine

2 tablespoons garlic salt

½ teaspoon ground black pepper

½ teaspoon ground white pepper

1 teaspoon ground cinnamon

½ teaspoon ground nutmeg

½ teaspoon ground allspice

½ teaspoon ground cloves

1 teaspoon sweet paprika

1 (16-ounce) package sliced mozzarella cheese

12 brioche hamburger buns

2 (16-ounce) jars pickled onions, drained

1½ cups pizza sauce, warmed

Steps:

1. In a medium bowl, combine pork and cooking wine and mix well. Set aside.

2. In a separate medium bowl, combine all dry seasonings, mixing well. Add mixture to the bowl with pork and mix well, making sure seasonings are completely mixed throughout the pork.

3. Preheat grill over medium heat.

4. Make 12 burgers out of the pork mixture and place on grill. Cook over medium heat with lid closed for 6 minutes, then flip over and continue cooking for another 6 minutes. Turn off heat and place a cheese slice onto each burger. Let stand for 2 minutes with lid closed to melt cheese.

5. Layer each bun with cudighi burger, pickled onions, and 2 tablespoons warmed pizza sauce. Serve.

Gideon's Buffalo Chicken Strip Sandwiches

I walked into the kitchen one day, and Gideon had the counter full of ingredients to make these sandwiches. Of course I was curious, so I whipped out my handy yellow notebook, where I write out all of my recipes, meal ideas, and grocery lists, and I wrote down everything he did. My children amaze me with how they can just grab different foods and create unique and super yummy meals. I think they feel so comfortable in the kitchen because I didn't mind them messing up my kitchen and cooking what they wanted when they were little.

Prep Time: 20 minutes
Cook Time: 25 minutes
Yields: 10 servings

Ingredients:

2 cups Frank's RedHot Original Cayenne Pepper Sauce

1 tablespoon salt

2 teaspoons ground black pepper

2 teaspoons paprika

1 tablespoon garlic powder

1 tablespoon onion powder

1/4 cup avocado oil (or olive oil)

2 (3-pound) bags frozen chicken tenderloins, thawed

10 sweet Hawaiian hamburger buns

1/4 cup salted butter, melted

2 tablespoons dried parsley

2 tablespoons garlic salt

1/2 cup unsalted butter

2 tablespoons minced fresh garlic

1 1/4 cups ranch dressing

1 (16-ounce) package sliced pepper jack cheese

4 large tomatoes, sliced thin

1 head iceberg lettuce, sliced thin

Steps:

1. In a large bowl, combine hot sauce, salt, pepper, paprika, garlic powder, onion powder, and oil. Whisk together and then add chicken to the bowl and coat well. Set aside.

2. Preheat oven to 375°F.

3. Separate buns and place them on ungreased 18" × 26" baking sheets with insides facing up. Brush insides of buns with 1/4 cup melted butter and sprinkle with parsley and garlic salt. Bake for 10 minutes or until the edges brown. Remove, then set aside.

4. In a large saucepan over medium heat, melt 1/2 cup unsalted butter and add minced garlic. Remove chicken from marinade and add to saucepan. Continue cooking for 6 minutes, then flip over and cook for 6 more minutes, until chicken is fully cooked.

5. Layer one half of each bun with 1 tablespoon ranch dressing, chicken, slice of cheese, another 1 tablespoon ranch dressing, tomatoes, and lettuce. Close buns and serve.

Lemon Pepper–Crusted Whitefish *with* Grilled Veggies

Having kids who love to fish, and living by the biggest freshwater lake in Michigan, means our family eats lots and lots of all kinds of fish. My favorite fish is whitefish. It has a mild taste and goes well with so many different spices. It is so versatile—whether you bake it, grill it, or fry it in a cast iron pan, it tastes great. During the summer months we do quite a bit of grilling, and with all the fish my boys catch for me to grill, whitefish is on the top of the list.

Prep Time: 25 minutes
Cook Time: 20 minutes
Yields: 10 servings

Ingredients:

1$\frac{1}{2}$ cups shredded Parmesan cheese

2 teaspoons plus 1 tablespoon garlic salt, divided

3 teaspoons ground black pepper, divided

4 tablespoons lemon pepper seasoning, divided

2 tablespoons dried parsley

$\frac{1}{2}$ cup almond meal

$\frac{1}{4}$ cup olive oil

10 (6–8 ounce) whitefish filets

1 cup salted butter, sliced

3 bunches asparagus spears, ends trimmed

2 large sweet Vidalia onions, peeled and sliced

4 large red sweet peppers, seeded and sliced thin

Steps:

1. In a medium bowl, combine cheese, 2 teaspoons garlic salt, 1 teaspoon black pepper, 2 tablespoons lemon pepper seasoning, parsley, and almond meal. Whisk together and set aside.

2. Pour oil into another medium bowl and set aside.

3. Preheat grill over medium heat. Place greased tinfoil on grill grates.

4. Lay fish skin-side down on ungreased 18" × 26" baking sheets and rub a thin coat of oil on top of fish, then sprinkle generously with cheese mixture. Continue with all filets. Place filets on the foil-covered grill. Cook for 10 minutes with lid closed, remove from the grill, cover with tinfoil, and set aside.

5. Place new tinfoil on grill grates and place butter slices evenly throughout. Top slices with all veggies, sprinkle with remaining 1 tablespoon garlic salt, 2 teaspoons black pepper, and 2 tablespoons lemon pepper seasoning. Cook over medium heat for 10 minutes, turning veggies often. Remove veggies from heat and serve with whitefish.

CHAPTER 6

Mexican-Inspired Favorites

~ ✳ ~

Three years later, the boys became big brothers to Izabella, "Izzy," their new sister. She always pulled a stool beside Mom to help make dinner. Her favorite meal is tacos.

Izabella, Izzy for short, came into our home when she was only five months old, and she definitely changed the whole vibe of the house. I figured out very quickly that raising girls is very different from raising boys. Izzy right away made her way to the kitchen, and I could tell that she would grow up and work in the culinary industry. Even when she was younger, she had a way of presenting simple foods in a fancy way that made you feel special when she gave it to you. She found her niche immediately with Mexican-inspired dishes. She makes, hands down, the best carnitas with homemade guac and corn tortilla shells I have ever tasted. She is so comfortable in the kitchen, and I often find her playing around with spices and trying to create new dinner recipes for our family to try out.

Izzy had no idea that years ago when David was only seven years old, he prayed for a little sister. One night he came into my bedroom before bed and asked me if I could pray with him that God would bring him a little sister that looked just like him. So the two of us headed into his room and knelt by his bed, and of course his little brothers Joshua and Gideon wanted to pray with us. That night the four of us prayed that God would send him a little sister. He continued to pray this same prayer every night for months, and then late one night we got a call from a social worker that a five-month-old little girl needed a home right away. That night around midnight, the social worker walked into our home with this sweet baby girl with the biggest brown eyes I had ever seen, and her name was Izabella. I could tell she was not sure what was going on, and so I sat in a rocking chair all night rocking and singing to her so she would feel more comfortable and safe with me. The next morning, David came downstairs ready for breakfast. He walked into the kitchen and couldn't believe his eyes. After months of praying for a little sister, God had answered his prayers. It truly was the sweetest thing; his eyes were as big as softballs and his mouth was wide open. He was stunned to see this sweet little girl sitting at his table eating breakfast. He ran over to her, and she smiled and grabbed his curly hair; he just stared at her with this huge smile all through breakfast.

When Izzy came into our home, she had different sensory sensitivities, which meant that our meal recipes had to change yet again. She and Joshua both had food sensitivities, but they differed from one another, so the types of foods I had to stay away from increased, making it more challenging when preparing dinner for our growing family of six. I had to learn to cook meals that we all could enjoy without having to make too many different dinner plates, because let's face it, cooking six different meals, three times a day, is not realistic!

Unlike Joshua, Izzy loved to eat foods that were cold, and so this was the perfect opportunity to incorporate fresh salads and veggies that she could munch on not only at mealtimes but also at snack times throughout the day. I also started adding fruit salads as a side dish option at dinner for my family.

As Izzy grew, she became less sensitive to certain foods and ate more of what I do best—my dinner casseroles. She also started asking me if she could help me in the kitchen. She would grab a chair, slide it to the counter, and help with dinner. I could see that she was very confident in putting foods together all on her own. I made Izzy my official taste tester to sneak in bits of different types of foods for her to try when I was cooking, which I think helped her to be able to start eating more rich and full foods.

This chapter is all about the Mexican-themed recipes that my daughter Izzy has mastered over the years. To this day she isn't afraid to combine different flavors and spices. Actually, she is the one who encouraged me to take those lonely spices sitting in the very back of the cabinet collecting dust and figure out how to cook with them. A couple of the herbs I steered away from were parsley and cilantro because I just didn't know what dish to use them with. Now, parsley has become one of my staples and I use it in quite a few of my recipes. When she sees that I have used it in my dish, she laughs and tells me how proud she is of me to expand my spice choices. Honestly, I really do feel like she is a way better cook than I am: She has a vision of what she wants to make and how it will look before she even starts putting the meal together. She has a love for food, and now our entire family gets to benefit from Izzy's imaginative meals.

Izzy's Famous Carnitas *with* Homemade Guacamole

Izzy makes the best carnitas. Wanna know how I know that they're the best? Because her brothers will ask her every single week to please make them for dinner. She also makes sure to make a ton of them because the boys like to eat it for breakfast with scrambled eggs and at lunchtime. They also will take to-go containers after dinner to eat later that night because they know it's going to go fast. It seems like everyone is hiding some in the back of the fridge for the next day or so!

Prep Time: 40 minutes
Cook Time: 3 hours and **30** minutes
Yields: 10 servings

Carnitas Ingredients:

1 (4-pound) boneless pork shoulder butt roast

2 tablespoons smoked paprika

2 tablespoons dried minced onion

2 tablespoons garlic salt

4 (1-ounce) packets fajita seasoning

2 (2-ounce) packets onion soup mix

4 cups water

1 (40-count) package corn tortillas (yellow or white)

1 (10-ounce) package queso fresco, crumbled

1 bunch cilantro, chopped

Homemade Guacamole Ingredients:

5 large ripe avocados, pitted, peeled, and sliced

1 tablespoon chopped cilantro

2 medium limes, juiced

1 tablespoon garlic salt

2 tablespoons medium salsa

2 tablespoons sour cream

Steps:

1. **Make the Carnitas:** In a 10-quart slow cooker, add pork, paprika, minced onion, garlic salt, fajita seasoning, soup mix, and water. Cover and cook on high for 3 hours or until meat starts to fall off the bone. Shred and place cover back on.

2. On a large griddle greased with butter, place tortillas to warm and slightly brown on both sides, about 4 minutes per shell. Set aside.

3. **Make the Homemade Guacomole:** In a large bowl, combine all Homemade Guacamole ingredients. Mix and set aside.

4. To each tortilla, add shredded pork, queso fresco, and cilantro.

5. Serve with Homemade Guacamole.

Cast Iron Chicken Fajitas

When I was in college, one of my roommates was a wonderful cook and would make the best chicken fajitas for dinner for us, especially during exam time when we were super stressed. They were so amazing and super simple to make. She passed this recipe on to me and, of course, I made a couple Mama Bell tweaks. Now every time I make it for my family, it reminds me of my good ole college days and the late-night dinners during exam week.

Prep Time: 30 minutes
Cook Time: 40 minutes (**5** per fajita)
Yields: 12 servings

Ingredients:

2 medium sweet Vidalia onions, peeled and sliced

2 medium yellow bell peppers, seeded and sliced

1 medium orange bell pepper, seeded and sliced

1 tablespoon minced fresh garlic

1 tablespoon garlic salt

1 tablespoon dried parsley

1 cup Italian dressing, divided

4 boneless, skinless chicken breasts, sliced into $1\frac{1}{2}$" strips

$\frac{1}{2}$ cup salted butter, plus 2 tablespoons

12 medium flour tortillas

3 cups shredded fiesta blend cheese mix

4 cups sour cream

4 cups medium salsa

1 bunch cilantro, chopped

Steps:

1. In a large saucepan, combine onion, bell peppers, minced garlic, garlic salt, parsley, and $\frac{1}{2}$ cup dressing. Stir and cook over medium heat for 15 minutes. Set aside.

2. In a separate large pan, combine chicken and remaining $\frac{1}{2}$ cup dressing. Cook over medium heat for 15 minutes or until cooked through, stirring occasionally. Set aside.

3. Heat a large griddle over medium heat and grease with butter. Place a tortilla on griddle and cook until it starts to brown, then flip and repeat on other side, about 5 minutes total.

4. Sprinkle center of tortilla with $\frac{1}{4}$ cup cheese, pepper and onion mixture, and chicken. Fold over tortilla edges to seal, press down with a spatula to keep the top from opening, and cook for an additional 2 minutes.

5. Repeat with remaining tortillas, making sure to grease griddle before each new tortilla.

6. Serve with sour cream, salsa, and cilantro.

Baked Chicken Tacos

Izzy and I both like to try out new recipes on the family. She started to take over Taco Tuesdays quite a while ago. Several times when she wanted to cook, I had to leave the kitchen so she could surprise us all, including me. I would try to peek into the kitchen to see what she was cooking, but she would catch me every time. I can hear her say, "Mom, I know you're there!" I just can't take it not knowing what's being made in the kitchen without me. When she made these baked tacos, it was the first time I had ever tried them. So delish!

Prep Time: **20** minutes
Cook Time: **1** hour and **10** minutes
Yields: **10** servings (**4** tacos each)

Ingredients:

4 pounds boneless, skinless chicken breasts, sliced

1 tablespoon Himalayan salt

1 tablespoon ground black pepper

1 tablespoon chipotle seasoning

2 (1-ounce) packets taco seasoning

¼ cup avocado oil

1 medium yellow onion, peeled and diced

1 (15-ounce) can garlic fire-roasted tomatoes

1 (15-ounce) can black beans, drained

2 (20-count) boxes Stand 'N Stuff hard taco shells

4 cups shredded fiesta blend cheese mix

1 bunch cilantro, chopped

1 (6-ounce) can pitted black olives, chopped and drained

Steps:

1. Preheat oven to 375°F.

2. In an ungreased 4-quart casserole dish, layer bottom with chicken and then sprinkle with salt, pepper, chipotle seasoning, and taco seasoning.

3. Continue layering with oil, onion, tomatoes, and beans. Bake for 1 hour.

4. Once done, remove chicken, place in a large bowl, and shred with a hand mixer. Return to juices and mix well. Don't turn oven off.

5. In 2 ungreased 9" × 13" casserole dishes, line up taco shells, fill with chicken mixture, and top with cheese.

6. Bake for 10 minutes.

7. Remove from oven, top with cilantro and olives, and serve.

Fiesta Fritos Bake

This recipe is so easy to make, and my kids really, really love this dinner. We are fans of the chili cheese corn chips, and instead of making a crust for this recipe I tried using the corn chips instead. It reminds me of a mix between a thick taco chili and a Tex-Mex goulash but without the noodles. This recipe will definitely be a favorite for Taco Tuesday. Another great idea is to use the corn chip dippers—they are wider and bigger and can cover the bottom faster with fewer chips.

Prep Time: 30 minutes
Cook Time: 35 minutes
Yields: 12 servings

Ingredients:

4 pounds 90/10 lean ground beef

1 tablespoon onion powder

1 tablespoon garlic powder

1 tablespoon chili powder

2 (1-ounce) packets taco seasoning

1 large yellow onion, peeled and diced

1 (15-ounce) can tomato sauce

1 (16-ounce) bag frozen corn

1 (15.5-ounce) can pinto beans, drained

1 (16-ounce) can red beans, drained

1 cup medium salsa

1 (4.5-ounce) can chopped green chilies

2 (9.25-ounce) bags chili cheese corn chips

4 cups shredded fiesta blend cheese mix

1 (8-ounce) container sour cream

2 cups pitted and chopped black olives

4 large tomatoes, chopped

4 cups shredded iceberg lettuce

Steps:

1. Preheat oven to 375°F.

2. In a large saucepan, combine beef, seasonings, and onions. Cook over medium heat for 15 minutes or until cooked through, stirring occasionally.

3. Add tomato sauce, corn, pinto beans, red beans, salsa, and green chilies. Stir together and set aside.

4. In 2 ungreased 10" × 15" casserole dishes, layer corn chips, 2 cups cheese, and meat mixture.

5. Top with remaining 2 cups cheese and bake for 20 minutes.

6. Serve with sour cream, olives, tomatoes, and lettuce on top.

Cast Iron Enchilada Bake

Whenever we go out for Mexican food, we go to a local, family-owned restaurant in our town that makes amazing enchiladas. I order the same exact thing every single time we go there—chicken and spinach enchiladas. Well, they inspired me to come home and create my own cast iron enchilada dish. I'm all about the red sauce and how when it cooks into the corn tortilla, it turns everything into a whole new texture. I think if I could, I would make enchiladas every other day for dinner.

Prep Time: 35 minutes
Cook Time: 2 hours and **15** minutes
Yields: 14 servings

Ingredients:

4 pounds 90/10 lean ground beef
2 (1-ounce) packets taco seasoning
1 tablespoon ground white pepper
1 tablespoon garlic powder
1 tablespoon minced fresh garlic
1 tablespoon dried minced onion
4 tablespoons avocado oil
20 white corn tortillas
1 (28-ounce) can red enchilada sauce
2 (15-ounce) jars medium salsa
2 (4.5-ounce) cans chopped green chilies
6 cups shredded medium Cheddar cheese
2 cups sour cream
2 (15-ounce) cans black beans, drained
4 cups fresh spinach leaves, chopped
1 cup shredded iceberg lettuce
2 (6-ounce) cans sliced black olives, drained

Steps:

1. Preheat oven to 375°F.

2. In a large stockpot combine beef and seasonings. Cook over medium heat for 15 minutes or until cooked through, stirring often. Set aside.

3. In a large frying pan over medium-low heat, add about 1 tablespoon oil, coating entire pan. Place in 1 tortilla at a time, warming each side for 2 minutes. Tortilla will soften. Repeat for all tortillas.

4. In a 17" round cast iron pan, add 1 cup enchilada sauce and 1 cup salsa. Spread over the entire bottom of pan. Place an even layer of tortillas, slightly overlapping edges.

5. Layer pan with meat, chilies, 2 cups cheese, remaining salsa, sour cream, beans, and spinach.

6. Continue layering with 2 more cups cheese, tortillas, remaining enchilada sauce, and last 2 cups cheese.

7. Bake for 40 minutes. Top with lettuce and olives and serve.

Walking Taco Casserole *with* Homemade Nacho Sauce

At every sporting event or fair, you find people selling walking tacos. It's this tiny bag of chips with a bunch of toppings stuffed into it. I love them too, but what a mess it is once you get done! Well, this walking taco casserole is the same concept but without all the cheesy fingers and food falling on the ground while you try to eat. This recipe was my first attempt at homemade nacho sauce and woo wee! It is wonderful!

Prep Time: 30 minutes
Cook Time: 30 minutes
Yields: 12 servings

Taco Meat Ingredients:

4 pounds 90/10 lean ground beef

4 (1-ounce) packets taco seasoning

Homemade Nacho Sauce Ingredients:

1/4 cup salted butter

1/2 cup all-purpose flour

1 cup whole milk

1 teaspoon garlic salt

2 cups shredded medium Cheddar cheese

2 teaspoons chopped green chilies

Additional Ingredients:

1 (9.25-ounce) bag nacho cheese tortilla chips

1 (9.25-ounce) bag corn chips

2 cups shredded fiesta blend cheese mix

1 (8-ounce) bag shredded iceberg lettuce

1 (8-ounce) container sour cream

1 (16-ounce) jar medium taco sauce

1 (6-ounce) can sliced black olives, drained

Steps:

1. **Make the Taco Meat:** In a large frying pan, combine beef and taco seasoning. Cook over medium heat for 15 minutes or until cooked through, stirring often. Set aside.

2. **Make the Homemade Nacho Sauce:** In a medium saucepan, combine butter and flour. Cook over medium heat for 5 minutes, whisking, and once it starts to bubble, whisk until a paste forms.

3. Slowly add milk while whisking. Once thickened, add garlic salt, Cheddar, and chilies. Stir and set aside.

4. In 2 ungreased 9" × 13" casserole dishes, layer tortilla chips and corn chips.

5. Next layer with beef, fiesta blend cheese, Homemade Nacho Sauce, lettuce, sour cream, taco sauce, and olives. Serve.

Blooming Quesadilla

This is probably one of the most fun dinners I've constructed for our family. For a while Izzy and I were all about Mexican-inspired dishes. We were really into finding ways to create super cool recipes for our Taco Tuesdays. We found this and knew we had to deconstruct it and create our own recipe. We were so excited to head to the grocery store to buy all the ingredients. I think we actually woke up while it was still dark to head into town for a coffee and a trip to the grocery store. It truly was a blast making this with her.

Prep Time: 40 minutes
Cook Time: 45 minutes
Yields: 16 servings

Ingredients:

4 pounds boneless, skinless chicken breasts

1 tablespoon each of minced fresh garlic, dried minced onion, garlic powder, chili powder, smoked paprika, and onion powder

$\frac{1}{2}$ tablespoon cayenne pepper

2 tablespoons ground cumin

1 large yellow bell pepper, seeded and chopped

1 large sweet Vidalia onion, peeled and chopped

2 (15-ounce) cans black beans, drained

2 cups taco sauce, divided

2 cups medium salsa, divided

16 large flour tortillas, cut into halves

1 bunch cilantro, chopped

4 cups queso fresco, crumbled

6 cups shredded fiesta blend cheese mix

Steps:

1. In a large saucepan, combine chicken, seasonings, bell pepper, and chopped onion. Cook over medium heat for 20 minutes or until fully cooked, stirring occasionally.

2. Remove chicken from pan and shred using a hand mixer. Return to pan and mix well. Add beans, 1 cup taco sauce, and 1 cup salsa. Mix again.

3. Preheat oven to 375°F.

4. Place a cut tortilla on a work surface, with the cut surface closest to you. Add $\frac{1}{4}$ cup chicken mixture to one side of cut tortilla. Sprinkle with cilantro and queso fresco cheese. Starting from the side with the meat, roll the tortilla up forming a cone shape. Place on an 18" × 26" baking sheet in a circle, small end of the cone facing inward. Repeat until a complete circle is formed. Sprinkle entire layer with 3 cups of fiesta cheese and remaining 1 cup salsa.

5. Repeat with remaining tortilla halves and layer on top of first circle, forming another circle on top. Sprinkle with remaining 3 cups fiesta cheese and drizzle with remaining 1 cup taco sauce.

6. Bake for 25 minutes. Tortillas should be crispy with edges that are nice and brown. Pull apart and enjoy.

Mexican Lasagna

My boys love lasagna for dinner, in fact when they come in after work and school they will literally dance in the kitchen when they see the huge lasagna. I already make a traditional lasagna and a breakfast lasagna, so I had to come up with a Mexican lasagna too. This dinner is super versatile, and you can add to it to make it your own. If you want to change it up you could add pulled pork or ground beef mixed with ground pork; both will turn out just as good as using chicken.

Prep Time: 30 minutes

Cook Time: 1 hour and **5** minutes

Yields: 12 servings

Ingredients:

4 pounds boneless, skinless chicken breasts

$\frac{1}{2}$ cup salted butter

1 tablespoon minced fresh garlic

1 tablespoon onion powder

1 tablespoon smoked paprika

2 tablespoons ground cumin

1 tablespoon garlic salt

1 tablespoon ground white pepper

1 (7-ounce) can chipotle peppers, diced

3 (15-ounce) cans black beans, drained

2 (16-ounce) jars medium salsa

2 (9-ounce) boxes oven-ready lasagna noodles

4 (15-ounce) cans garlic fire-roasted tomatoes, drained

6 cups shredded fiesta blend cheese mix

2 (8-ounce) containers sour cream

Steps:

1. In a large frying pan, add chicken, butter, garlic, and dry seasonings. Cook over medium heat for 15 minutes, stirring occasionally.

2. Reduce heat to low and add chipotle peppers, beans, and salsa. Simmer for 15 minutes or until cooked through, stirring a few times.

3. Remove chicken from pan and use a hand mixer to shred chicken. Return to pan and stir together.

4. Preheat oven to 375°F.

5. Layer an ungreased 5-quart casserole dish with noodles, half of the chicken mixture, 2 cans tomatoes, and 3 cups cheese. Repeat layers, ending with cheese. Cover with tinfoil and place in oven.

6. Bake for 35 minutes. Top with sour cream and serve.

Cast Iron Taco Ring

Am I the only one that finds something cool to make for dinner, then makes it over and over again with different ingredients just to see if it will taste as yummy as the original? One summer I was all about the crescent roll ring meal. I stuffed it full of so many different foods. I love the way it looks when it's finished and ready to serve; it makes me feel like a professional chef (and it impressed my eight kids at the same time!). When my dinners look picture-perfect, it's just so hard for me to cut into it and serve. They're just too beautiful to eat.

Prep Time: 35 minutes
Cook Time: 55 minutes
Yields: 10 servings

Ingredients:

2 pounds 90/10 lean ground beef

2 (1-ounce) packets taco seasoning

1 tablespoon minced fresh garlic

2 tablespoons dried minced onion

1 tablespoon smoked paprika

2 (4-ounce) cans chopped green chilies

4 (8-ounce) tubes refrigerated crescent rolls

2 (15-ounce) cans refried beans

2 (15-ounce) cans black beans, drained

3 cups shredded medium Cheddar cheese, divided

½ cup salted butter, melted

1 tablespoon dried parsley

1 (8-ounce) container sour cream

1 (15-ounce) jar medium salsa

1 (15-ounce) can sliced black olives, drained

1 (8-ounce) bag shredded iceberg lettuce

4 medium tomatoes, diced

Steps:

1. Preheat oven to 375°F.

2. In a large saucepan, combine beef, taco seasoning, garlic, minced onion, paprika, and chilies. Cook over medium heat for 15 minutes or until cooked through, stirring occasionally. Set aside.

3. In the middle of a 17" round cast iron pan, place a small bowl upside down. Open tubes of crescent rolls. Roll out dough and separate into triangles. Place the wide end of dough toward the small bowl, continuing around the pan and making sure to overlap each section about ½" and to drape the pointed end over the edge of the pan. Then, remove bowl and press bottom of crusts to seal.

4. Layer inside of dough with refried beans, making sure to spread out evenly. Next, top with beef, black beans, and 2 cups cheese. Take triangles draping over side of pan and pull over filling, tucking it under dough on other side and pressing to seal. Repeat for all triangles. Brush with melted butter and sprinkle with parsley.

5. Bake for 40 minutes, or until golden. Sprinkle with remaining cup cheese. Serve with sour cream, salsa, olives, lettuce, and tomatoes.

White Chicken Enchiladas

I grew up with my mom making this dish often for us eight kids. I felt like whenever she made this it was a special dinner. She presented it like it came from a fancy restaurant, at least that's how I felt being only eight years old. The best memories I have are of my beautiful mom coming to the table with a huge pan or dish of the best dinner ever. She'd have a huge smile on her face, probably because she could see our eyes get so big waiting to see what she'd made for dinner that day.

Prep Time: 30 minutes
Cook Time: 1 hour and **30** minutes
Yields: 12 servings

Ingredients:

8 tablespoons olive oil, divided

4 pounds boneless, skinless chicken breasts, cut into $1/2$" cubes

2 tablespoons minced fresh garlic

1 tablespoon dried minced onion

1 tablespoon garlic powder

$1/2$ tablespoon ground white pepper

1 tablespoon chopped fresh parsley

1 (22.6-ounce) can condensed cream of mushroom soup

1 (27-ounce) can chopped green chilies

1 (8-ounce) container sour cream

1 (30-count) package corn tortillas (yellow or white)

4 cups shredded white Cheddar cheese

2 bunches green onions, ends trimmed, chopped

Steps:

1. Preheat oven to 375°F.

2. In a large skillet, heat 4 tablespoons oil over medium heat. Add chicken, minced garlic, minced onion, garlic powder, pepper, and parsley. Sauté for 20 minutes.

3. Fold in soup, chilies, and sour cream. Mix well and set aside.

4. In a separate large skillet heat 1 tablespoon oil over medium heat. In batches, cook tortillas for 2–3 minutes on each side until browned. Add more oil to the pan as needed.

5. Layer 2 ungreased 10" × 15" casserole dishes with tortillas (lying flat, overlapping if necessary), chicken mixture, cheese, and green onions. Repeat layers in each casserole so that there are two layers in each dish.

6. Bake for 35 minutes and serve.

Fresh Corn *and* Black Bean Salsa

Every summer we plant a huge garden. Normally, I preserve and can all my veggies, salsas, jams, and relishes so we can enjoy them throughout the fall, winter, and spring months. And one of the family's favorite dishes is this fresh garden salsa. When my husband sees the ingredients on the counter, he knows the salsa is going to be ready for eating. Knowing that he really enjoys fresh salsa, I will keep a container aside so he can enjoy it at nighttime, sitting in his favorite "Dad chair." Serve this with tortilla chips or add to your favorite Mexican recipes.

Prep Time: 45 minutes
Cook Time: N/A
Yields: 8 pints

Ingredients:

20 large ripe tomatoes, diced

2 large yellow onions, peeled and chopped

4 large green bell peppers, seeded and chopped

2 medium jalapeño peppers, carefully seeded and diced (wash hands after handling)

16 cloves garlic, peeled and diced

2 cups uncooked fresh corn

2 (15-ounce) cans black beans, drained

1 cup chopped cilantro

1 cup apple cider vinegar

4 tablespoons fresh lime juice

2 tablespoons Himalayan salt

1 tablespoon ground black pepper

2 tablespoons white sugar

2 tablespoons garlic salt

3 tablespoons ground cumin

1 cup chopped green onions

1 tablespoon smoked paprika

Steps:

1. In a large bowl, combine all ingredients in order listed and stir to combine.

2. Cover and let sit for 24 hours in the fridge to allow juices and flavors to come out, or eat fresh right away if desired.

CHAPTER 7

Super-Easy Slow Cooker Meals

~ ✳ ~

Hailey came into their lives. She'd prayed to have a big family, to live on a farm, and to go to church. She introduced Mom to making big meals in a slow cooker.

In my pantry I had two beautiful slow cookers just waiting to be used. My mother and sister use theirs so much that they have had to replace them several times, and here I sat with two still in the box. I used to think that slow cookers are one of those cooking appliances that everyone has in their home but only brings out during the holidays. To me, unless it's for little sausages smothered in barbecue sauce or cheese dip for tortilla chips, that slow cooker is staying in the box.

However, one day not too long ago, my daughter Hailey walked up the stairs with my slow cooker. My first thought was, "Whose slow cooker is that?" I soon realized that it was mine from my wedding twenty-four years ago, and no lie, she *really* had to look hard to find it way up in the very back of my pantry. She had been seeing slow cooker recipes online and wanted to try her hand at making one. The first meal she made was a chicken pasta dish and it was absolutely *amazing*. I asked her if she would like to make a slow cooker meal every week, and she was excited to start putting together her own creations for us to try. I was so impressed by her meals that she literally dumped into the cooker and left cooking for the day. Immediately, the wheels began to turn in my head, and cooking with a slow cooker began to make sense, especially when cooking for a big family like ours. Right away I ordered

Hailey the biggest slow cooker I could find so she could make even bigger meals.

Hailey has come so far since she moved into our home. I still remember the day our phone rang two weeks before Christmas, and on the phone was our friend who was also the social worker who brought each of our children into our home. She started the conversation off by saying, "Congratulations, you have a girl!" I was so confused, and she proceeded to tell me that she had a nine-year-old girl currently in foster care that was looking for a forever home and she wants to live on a farm, go to church, and have a big family. Plus, our friend is bringing her over to the house that week so we could meet her, and if everything goes well, they would like her to move in after Christmas. I was pretty excited and had big plans to make Christmas cookies with her, but right away she asked David if they could go to the barn and see the horses. My plan didn't go like I'd wanted, but David and Hailey instantly formed a bond and became the best of friends. Before she moved in, Izzy could not wait to have a big sister to share her room with her. We got a bed for Hailey all set up, and Izzy helped me clean the room and even shared her stuffed animals by putting some on Hailey's pillow, hoping it would help her adjust easier when she came to live with us.

Hailey loved the animals in the barn, and Dad bought her a goat that had twin kids, plus he gave her a Clydesdale horse of her own named Daisy Duke. Hailey still has her today, and she had a foal named Dolly. Even though Hailey was adopted, she is exactly like me, 100 percent. We have the same temperament, dress the same, and both enjoy the beach. It's amazing how God works and knew that we needed each other. She is my partner when shopping, cleaning, and cooking. She has been our main farm girl since the minute she became part of our family. I truly can't imagine my life without her in it.

I feel Hailey really struggled the most with my meals; she wasn't used to eating veggies right out of the garden and didn't like me adding any kind of spices. I addressed meals a little differently than I did with my other children. Instead of making different meals, I would just take some out for Hailey and set it aside before I added the spices, but as she got older she became the one that thinks, "the spicier the better." Patience and not forcing foods on her helped her to embrace new foods and become more comfortable in the kitchen.

This chapter belongs to Hailey because I'm just so proud of who she has grown into. She is a wonderful young lady, and I am so excited that she took it upon herself to dig out the ole slow cooker and experiment with spices that she would never touch when she was little. There hasn't been a meal yet that she's made that I haven't loved and had to write down in my favorite recipes notebook. Whenever I share her slow cooker recipes online, her videos go viral. People are always asking for her to share another recipe for them to try with their families. These meals are great for families who are always on the go or for working folks who need to throw everything together and let it slow cook all day so dinner is ready when everyone comes home. 🌹

Hailey's Slow Cooker Chicken Alfredo

Chicken Alfredo is one of those meals that can be put together fast. It's a simple meal that doesn't take a lot of time to make, and it turns out great no matter what ingredients you add to the chicken. Whether it's broccoli, carrots, or some fried-up bacon added in, it will still be delicious. Once you tackle the cream sauce, you can add your special touches. This is one of those meals that my son Gideon always asks to be put on our weekly menu board.

Prep Time: 10 minutes
Cook Time: 4–5 hours
Yields: 10 servings

Ingredients:

4 pounds boneless, skinless chicken breasts, sliced into strips

3 tablespoons avocado oil

1 tablespoon minced fresh garlic

1 teaspoon garlic powder

1 teaspoon salt

1 teaspoon ground black pepper

1 tablespoon dried Italian seasoning

2$\frac{1}{2}$ cups heavy cream, divided

1 cup salted butter

1 (8-ounce) block cream cheese

1 (16-ounce) box rigatoni pasta, uncooked

1 cup chicken broth

2 cups shredded Parmesan cheese

Steps:

1. In a 10-quart slow cooker, add chicken, oil, and seasonings. Stir to completely coat chicken.

2. Add 2 cups heavy cream, butter, and cream cheese and stir. Cover and cook on high for 3–4 hours or until chicken is completely cooked through.

3. Once chicken is cooked through, add pasta, broth, and remaining $\frac{1}{2}$ cup heavy cream and give it a stir.

4. Cover, reduce heat to low, and cook until pasta is soft, approximately 1 hour.

5. Once done, top with Parmesan and serve!

Slow Cooker Parmesan Chicken *and* Potatoes

This was one of the first slow cooker meals Hailey made for us. It's the perfect meal to try out on our family because it has two of our favorite food items: yellow potatoes and chicken. Every summer we plant yellow potatoes in our huge garden, so this dish was extra yummy because of the fresh garden potatoes that she used. We love potatoes so much that I plant at least fifty plants, which will yield almost three hundred potatoes to can for the winter and cook fresh during the summer and fall months.

Prep Time: 30 minutes
Cook Time: 4 hours
Yields: 10 servings

Ingredients:

3 tablespoons avocado oil, divided

10 yellow potatoes, cut into 2" cubes

½ cup salted butter, divided

4 tablespoons minced fresh garlic, divided

1 tablespoon dried parsley flakes

2 teaspoons salt, divided

2 teaspoons ground black pepper

2 cups shredded Parmesan cheese, divided

4 pounds boneless, skinless chicken breasts, sliced in half

Steps:

1. In a 10-quart slow cooker, drizzle 2 tablespoons oil and toss in potatoes, making sure to completely coat. Add in ¼ cup butter, 1 tablespoon garlic, parsley, 1 teaspoon salt, 1 teaspoon pepper, and 1 cup cheese. Mix together.

2. In a medium bowl, add chicken, remaining 1 teaspoon salt, 1 teaspoon pepper, and 1 tablespoon oil and coat well.

3. Place chicken on top of potato mixture and top with remaining ¼ cup butter, 3 tablespoons garlic, and 1 cup cheese.

4. Cover and cook on low for 4 hours or until chicken is completely cooked through. Serve.

Slow Cooker Peanut Butter Chicken Stir-Fry

Peanut butter is my son Robert's and my favorite condiment of all time! I'm constantly looking for ways to use peanut butter, whether in peanut butter cookies, dinner recipes, or smothered on toast. I even love the smell of peanut butter, that's how much I love it. You're probably thinking to yourself, "Can someone actually love peanut butter that much?" The answer is a confident yes, and her name is Heather Bell, a.k.a. Mama Bell. Needless to say, this is one of my favorite recipes because the key ingredient is, you guessed it, peanut butter!

Prep Time: 10 minutes
Cook Time: 5–6 hours
Yields: 10 servings

Ingredients:

3 pounds boneless, skinless chicken breasts, cut into 1" cubes

2 cups creamy peanut butter

2 tablespoons minced fresh garlic

4 tablespoons fresh lime juice

4 tablespoons liquid aminos (or soy sauce)

2 tablespoons pure maple syrup

2 cups water

2 cups chopped fresh broccoli

2 cups thinly sliced baby bella mushrooms

1 medium yellow bell pepper, seeded and sliced thin

1 medium red bell pepper, seeded and sliced thin

1 medium green bell pepper, seeded and sliced thin

2 (15-ounce) cans baby corn, drained

2 cups frozen peas

2 (14-ounce) cans bean sprouts, drained

2 (5-ounce) cans sliced water chestnuts, drained

2 (8-ounce) jars pad thai sauce

4 cups cooked white rice

1 (14-ounce) package chow mein noodles

Steps:

1. In a 10-quart slow cooker, add chicken, peanut butter, garlic, lime juice, liquid aminos, maple syrup, and water. Cover and cook on low for 4–5 hours or until chicken is completely cooked through.

2. Remove lid and add all veggies, bean sprouts, water chestnuts, and pad thai sauce. Stir well and cook for 1 more hour.

3. Once the veggies are tender, stir once more.

4. Serve over rice and top with chow mein noodles.

Slow Cooker Tuscan Chicken *and* Pasta

This dinner is one of my all-time favorite meals that I have made in a slow cooker. I planted dozens of Roma tomatoes in my garden because I wanted to try and make sun-dried tomatoes for the very first time. Let me tell you what! They turned out amazing, and I couldn't wait to add them to a recipe to see how they tasted. Using them as the star of the meal was perfect. I reserved the oil to add to the chicken to help give it extra flavor. My son Gideon literally had four helpings, and if I hadn't stopped him he probably would have licked the pot clean.

Prep Time: 20 minutes
Cook Time: 3–4 hours
Yields: 10 servings

Ingredients:

4 pounds boneless, skinless chicken breasts, sliced thin

2 tablespoons avocado oil

1 (8-ounce) jar sun-dried tomatoes, drained (oil reserved)

1 teaspoon salt

1 teaspoon ground black pepper

1 tablespoon dried Italian seasoning

1 tablespoon paprika

1 teaspoon garlic salt

1 teaspoon ground white pepper

1 tablespoon minced fresh garlic

2 cups heavy cream

2 cups Italian shredded cheese mix

2 cups chopped fresh spinach leaves

1 (16-ounce) box penne pasta, cooked

Steps:

1. In a 10-quart slow cooker, add chicken, avocado oil, and oil from sun-dried tomato jar. Coat chicken well, then sprinkle with salt, black pepper, Italian seasoning, and paprika.

2. In a medium bowl, combine sun-dried tomatoes, garlic salt, white pepper, minced garlic, cream, cheese, and spinach. Stir and add to chicken. Be sure to spread out evenly.

3. Cover and cook on high for 3–4 hours or until chicken is completely cooked through. Once chicken is done, transfer chicken to a large bowl and shred with a hand mixer. Return chicken to the cooker and add cooked penne. Stir again and serve!

Slow Cooker Chicken Cordon Bleu

This recipe is similar to the traditional cordon bleu but of course in a slow cooker. I remember that when I was younger, my dad made cordon bleu for dinner and I couldn't get enough of that creamy Swiss cheese sauce poured over the chicken and ham. I was always the first one at the table with a fork in hand waiting for my plate, and I would hurry up and eat it so I could get seconds. This dish is inspired by my dad, who passed away several years ago, and when I make this it brings back a flood of great memories that I will always cherish.

Prep Time: 10 minutes
Cook Time: 4–5 hours
Yields: 10 servings

Ingredients:

2 tablespoons avocado oil

4 pounds boneless, skinless chicken breasts, sliced thin

1 tablespoon dried parsley

1 tablespoon dried thyme

1 tablespoon garlic powder

1 teaspoon salt

1 teaspoon ground black pepper

2 tablespoons minced fresh garlic

2 cups chicken broth

2 (8-ounce) packages shredded Swiss cheese

1 (8-ounce) block cream cheese

1 (16-ounce) package sliced black forest ham, chopped

1 (16-ounce) box penne pasta, uncooked

1 (8-ounce) container sour cream

Steps:

1. In a 10-quart slow cooker, add oil, chicken, and seasonings. Stir well to coat chicken.

2. Add broth, Swiss cheese, and cream cheese and stir. Cover and cook on low for 3–4 hours.

3. Once chicken is cooked through, add chopped ham, pasta, and sour cream. Stir again, then cover and continue cooking for 1 hour more or until pasta is tender. Serve.

Noah's Slow Cooker Chili Beefy Mac

My son Noah has become quite the cook. I really love when my children ask to make dinner to give me a break. When they cook dinner, I just grab a cup of coffee and watch them cook. My kitchen is my happy place, and it makes my heart happy knowing that they are so comfortable cooking for our big family. Plus, I think it gives them more confidence that I'm close by if they have any questions or need some suggestions from Mom. Noah did a terrific job on this Slow Cooker Chili Beefy Mac.

Prep Time: 20 minutes
Cook Time: 2 hours and **25** minutes
Yields: 10 servings

Ingredients:

3 pounds 90/10 lean ground beef

1 tablespoon minced fresh garlic

1 tablespoon dried minced onion

1 medium sweet Vidalia onion, peeled and diced

1 tablespoon chili powder

1 tablespoon dried oregano

1 tablespoon paprika

4 cups beef broth

1 (16-ounce) box elbow pasta, uncooked

2 (16-ounce) cans chili beans

3 (24-ounce) jars spaghetti sauce

3 cups shredded medium Cheddar cheese

1 (8-ounce) bag corn chips

1 (8-ounce) container sour cream

Steps:

1. In a large skillet, cook beef over medium heat for 15 minutes. Add garlic, minced onion, and diced onion, then continue cooking for 10 minutes or until cooked through, stirring occasionally.

2. In a 10-quart slow cooker, add meat mixture, chili powder, oregano, paprika, broth, and pasta. Stir together. Cover and cook on high for 1 hour or until pasta is tender.

3. Add beans, spaghetti sauce, and cheese. Stir and cover. Continue cooking for another hour.

4. Serve with corn chips on the bottom of a bowl and sour cream on top.

Izzy's Slow Cooker Taco Chili

Living so far up north, we eat quite a bit of chili because it is not uncommon that we have -10°F temperatures for weeks and then maybe hit 20°F. So, I like to make chili for my family because they work outside, and I want to make something hearty and warm. I am always looking for different ways to make chili, and Izzy's Slow Cooker Taco Chili recipe absolutely didn't disappoint. It's like Taco Tuesday and Chili Weekends all wrapped up into one amazing meal. Plus, it's so easy to make that I find myself using this as a go-to recipe for when I am stuck on what to serve my family.

Prep Time: 30 minutes
Cook Time: 3–4 hours
Yields: 10 servings

Ingredients:

3 pounds 90/10 lean ground turkey

6 teaspoons salt, divided

2 teaspoons ground black pepper, divided

6 teaspoons ground cumin, divided

6 teaspoons ground coriander, divided

1 large yellow onion, peeled and chopped

2 (29-ounce) cans tomato sauce

2 (29-ounce) cans black beans, drained

1 (29-ounce) can pinto beans, drained

2 tablespoons chili powder

4 cups shredded medium Cheddar cheese

1 bunch fresh cilantro, chopped

1 (11-ounce) bag tortilla chips

Steps:

1. In a large skillet, combine turkey, 2 teaspoons salt, 1 teaspoon pepper, 2 teaspoons cumin, 2 teaspoons coriander, and onion. Cook over medium heat for 20 minutes or until cooked through, stirring occasionally.

2. Transfer turkey mixture and drippings to a 10-quart slow cooker. Add tomato sauce, black beans, pinto beans, chili powder, and remaining seasonings. Stir well, then cover and cook on high for 3–4 hours until cooked through, making sure to check and stir often.

3. Once done, sprinkle with cheese, cilantro, and tortilla chips. Serve.

Slow Cooker Chicken, Bacon, *and* Ranch Pasta

This recipe is gonna be one that your family will ask for over and over. Bacon is one of the many staples in my pantry. My son Gideon puts ranch dressing on everything, and I mean everything! That got me thinking how great a slow cooker dish would be if I combined chicken with crispy bacon and ranch seasoning. It was a hit with my family.

Prep Time: 40 minutes
Cook Time: 3 hours and **50** minutes
Yields: 10 servings

Ingredients:

3 pounds boneless, skinless chicken breasts

2 cups chicken broth

1 tablespoon dried minced onion

1 tablespoon ground yellow mustard

2 tablespoons minced fresh garlic

2 teaspoons salt, divided

2 teaspoons ground black pepper, divided

1 (1-ounce) packet dry ranch seasoning mix

1 (8-ounce) block cream cheese, cubed

2 cups shredded medium Cheddar cheese

2 cups heavy cream

$1/2$ cup salted butter

1 pound bacon, chopped

2 cups peeled and chopped carrots

1 medium red onion, peeled and diced

1 (16-ounce) box penne pasta, uncooked

Steps:

1. In a 10-quart slow cooker, add chicken, broth, minced onion, mustard, garlic, 1 teaspoon salt, 1 teaspoon pepper, ranch seasoning, cream cheese, Cheddar, and heavy cream. Cover and cook on low for $2\frac{1}{2}$ hours.

2. Melt butter in a large skillet over medium-high heat. Add bacon, carrots, onion, and remaining 1 teaspoon salt and 1 teaspoon pepper and cook over medium-high heat for 15 minutes until bacon is done and veggies are tender, stirring occasionally.

3. Add bacon and veggies to slow cooker, stir together, and cook for another 35 minutes, covered.

4. Uncover the slow cooker and transfer chicken to a cutting board. Cut chicken into bite-sized pieces and return to slow cooker. Stir in penne, cover, and cook for an additional 30 minutes or until pasta is tender. Serve and enjoy!

Breakfast Slow Cooker Denver Omelet

We have made so many wonderful dinner recipes with the slow cooker that I had to try out breakfast. When I was growing up, my mom and dad made breakfast for dinner at least three times a week. Our family really loved breakfast foods. So to make a breakfast recipe and serve it to my family for dinner seemed like a super cool idea. They loved it! Now I make breakfast pizzas and biscuits and gravy quite a bit for dinner and this super delicious recipe too!

Prep Time: 15 minutes
Cook Time: 3–4 hours
Yields: 10 servings

Ingredients:

1 medium red bell pepper, seeded and chopped
1 medium green bell pepper, seeded and chopped
1 medium yellow onion, peeled and chopped
1 (16-ounce) package sliced black forest ham, chopped
10 large eggs
1 teaspoon Worcestershire sauce
1 teaspoon salt
1 teaspoon ground black pepper
1 tablespoon Dijon mustard
2 cups whole milk
2 tablespoons avocado oil
4 cups (1" cubes) French bread
2 cups shredded medium Cheddar cheese, divided

Steps:

1. In a medium bowl, combine red and green peppers, onion, and ham. Stir together and set aside.

2. In a separate medium bowl, combine eggs, Worcestershire sauce, salt, black pepper, mustard, and milk. Whisk together until lightly scrambled and set aside.

3. In a 10-quart slow cooker, spread oil on the bottom, then layer with 2 cups cubed bread, half of veggie and ham mixture, and ½ cup cheese.

4. Repeat the layers (bread, veggies and ham, ½ cup cheese) and then pour egg mixture over the top.

5. Cover and cook on low for 3–4 hours, until egg is cooked through.

6. When done, sprinkle remaining 1 cup cheese on top and serve.

Slow Cooker Crack Chicken

This recipe was the very first dinner Hailey made for our family. She said she wanted to make it all by herself without any tips or advice and surprise all of us at dinnertime. She went to the store and bought all the ingredients herself and wouldn't let me into the kitchen until it was completely finished. It was amazing. I'm so proud of her. Her sister and brothers ate every single bit of it and thanked her and asked when she would be cooking again.

Prep Time: 15 minutes
Cook Time: 4 hours
Yields: 10 servings

Ingredients:

2 tablespoons olive oil (or avocado oil)

5 pounds boneless, skinless chicken breasts

4 (8-ounce) blocks cream cheese, cubed

6 cups shredded medium Cheddar cheese

3 (1-ounce) packets dry ranch seasoning mix

5 cups water

4 cups uncooked instant white rice

Steps:

1. In a 10-quart slow cooker, place oil on the bottom. Then layer chicken, cream cheese, Cheddar, and ranch seasoning.

2. Cover and cook on low for 4 hours.

3. While chicken is cooking, use a medium saucepan to boil water and then add rice. Stir together and simmer on low for 10 minutes, covered. Remove lid and fluff with a fork, then set aside.

4. Remove chicken from slow cooker, shred with a hand mixer, and return to cooker.

5. Mix and serve chicken mixture over rice.

CHAPTER 8

The Bell Family's Favorite Cookies

~ ✱ ~

Three brothers came along, and the family knew immediately that they would complete the family. Robert *is the "cookie monster" because of his love for all kinds of Mom's cookies.*

Just when I thought our family was complete, along come the sweetest boys ever: Robert, the oldest, followed by his two younger brothers, Brendon and Noah. Before the boys moved into our house, they were our neighbors and would come over and have lunch and dinner with us. Robert really, really loves sweets, especially Nana's Famous Chocolate Chip Cookies. Every time he came over, he would look around the kitchen to see if I had made cookies. So, I started making cookies for him and would walk them over so they could enjoy them at home. He would open the door with a huge smile, knowing I was delivering his cookies, and he always made sure to thank me and bring the plate back, anxious for it to be filled again. When the boys were little, Robert was very protective of his brothers and made sure that no matter what they were always taken care of, even if it meant he had to make dinner, help dress them, and get them off to school. He had to grow up real fast because he was trying to help his mother and father out as much as he could. Just writing this makes me tear up thinking about how strong he had to be at such a young age. When I think of my son Robert, two words come to mind: courage and loyalty.

The youngest brother, Noah, was placed into our home; we were chosen because the brothers lived next door and the social worker wanted to keep the boys close together. Later that year, Robert and Brendon's father passed away suddenly. We all struggled with his death because he was not only the boys' father, but also a close friend of ours. We loved him like family, and he had also worked for our masonry company. He was a joy to be around and worked hard to take care of his boys. We loved all three of the boys so much and wanted them to stay together. We talked with some of the boys' close family members and then to the boys. We all agreed that they would come into our home and become part of our family. It was so important to us that we had the support of their family first and then the boys could choose for themselves where they would like to live. That next year, Robert, Brendon, and Noah became part of the Bell family.

Once the boys moved in, Robert was so helpful and stayed by my side all the time like he was "watching over me"; he would remind me of appointments, when activities started, and if we needed to get groceries. He was so used to taking care of everyone around him that I think he wasn't sure how to just be a kid. Once, on our way home from grocery shopping, he started reminding me of an event to come and I looked at him and said, "Robert, I love you and am very thankful you help me, but I will always take care of you and your brothers. You can now be the son and enjoy life—I got you." He just looked at me and tears began to roll down his face. You could see the relief in his face and the burden just lift away. This was one of the sweetest moments with Robert I will never forget.

Robert wasn't a picky eater; he gobbled everything I made for breakfast, lunch, and dinner. He couldn't wait for meals—he was so busy playing sports, and I swear he had the fastest metabolism ever.

But there was this one meal that I made, my homemade mac and cheese, that he took a bite of and gagged. (I was shocked to say the least, because everyone tells me my mac and cheese is amazing.) He spit it out and said that it was "too cheesy." That first year he gagged and spit out several of my homemade meals, so I had to backtrack and bring in some boxed foods that the boys were familiar with while still making some homemade items too. I hoped that by introducing a little bit of the homemade dishes, they would eventually enjoy my way of cooking and the spices I use consistently in my meals. Now years later when I ask my family what they want me to cook for the week, what's the one thing my Robert asks for every single week? Well, believe it or not, it's my homemade mac and cheese! Funny how he's changed his tune all these years later.

But one thing is for sure—he has always loved my plates of Nana's Famous Chocolate Chip Cookies, and that's why this chapter is dedicated to Robert. His favorite cookies are for sure chocolate chip cookies, but honestly, if "cookie" is in the name he'll pretty much eat them all.

The neatest thing is Robert and Brendon now live in our rental house, the same house that they lived in with their father when they were little. Now over ten years later I still bake cookies for both of them and walk across my yard, past the chicken barn, to take them over to their house. Robert will open the door with the same huge smile, but now instead of a simple thank you, I get a huge hug followed by, "Thanks, Mom, I love you."

Mama Bell's Fab Five Chocolate Chip Cookies

My regular chocolate chip cookies are great, but one day I decided to amp them up and go big or go home. So, I made this cookie with all kinds of delicious chocolate chips. I like to use a variety of chips to add different textures. There is nothing like biting into a warm chocolate chip cookie when the chocolate just drips out of the cookie, and then you grab a glass of cold milk out of the fridge and dip this monster of a cookie into it. This brings me back to when I was a kid and my mom made us cookies after school. When I bake, it brings back so many wonderful memories of my mother in the kitchen.

Prep Time: 30 minutes
Cook Time: 12 minutes per batch
Yields: 36 cookies

Ingredients:
½ cup salted butter, softened
½ cup shortening
1 cup packed light brown sugar
1 cup white sugar
2 large eggs, room temperature
2 teaspoons pure vanilla extract
3 cups all-purpose flour
½ cup unsweetened cocoa powder
1 (3.4-ounce) box chocolate instant pudding mix
1 teaspoon baking powder
1 teaspoon Himalayan salt
1 teaspoon instant coffee granules
1 cup dark chocolate chips
1 cup mini semisweet chocolate chips
1 cup semisweet chocolate chunks
½ cup milk chocolate chips
½ cup espresso chocolate chips

Steps:

1. Preheat oven to 350°F.

2. In a large mixing bowl, cream together butter, shortening, and both sugars for 5 minutes until light and fluffy. Add eggs and vanilla and continue mixing for another 5 minutes. Set aside.

3. In another large bowl, combine all remaining ingredients and whisk together.

4. Add half dry mixture to creamed mixture and combine until mixed through and then repeat with the other half.

5. Drop dough by tablespoonful onto ungreased 18" × 26" baking sheets, about 2" apart. Bake for 12 minutes or until the edges of the cookies start to brown. Cool cookies on the pan for 2 minutes and then transfer to a wire rack. Cool completely or serve warm.

White Chocolate Chip Banana Cookies

In the summer, one of the things I make often is chocolate chip banana bread. We eat a lot of bananas; for example, banana bread, banana pudding, and just plain bananas. With six boys in the gym lifting every day, we go through dozens of them each week. I decided to create a spin-off of my original chocolate cookies and make these white chocolate chip ones with a banana flavor. I decided to make them for Easter and added pastel, spring-colored sprinkles for extra color.

Prep Time: 30 minutes
Cook Time: 12 minutes per batch
Yields: 36 cookies

Ingredients:

⅔ cup salted butter, softened
⅔ cup shortening
1 cup packed light brown sugar
1 cup white sugar
2 large eggs, room temperature
2 teaspoons vanilla bean paste
1 medium banana, mashed
3 cups all-purpose flour
1 teaspoon Himalayan salt
1 teaspoon baking soda
1 (3.4-ounce) box banana instant pudding mix
1 (12-ounce) bag white chocolate chips
1 (12-ounce) bag peanut butter chips
1 (12-ounce) bag funfetti chips (or cheesecake chips)
1 (2-ounce) jar pastel sprinkles

Steps:

1. Preheat oven to 350°F.

2. In a large mixing bowl, cream butter and shortening together for 2 minutes until light and fluffy.

3. Add sugars, eggs, and vanilla. Mix for an additional 5 minutes. Fold banana into batter and mix well.

4. In a separate large bowl, combine flour, salt, baking soda, and pudding mix. Whisk together. Add half to cream mixture, mix until flour is completely combined, then add the other half and continue mixing until completely mixed through.

5. Add white chocolate chips, peanut butter chips, funfetti chips, and pastel sprinkles to batter and fold in with a wooden spoon.

6. Using a tablespoon, drop onto ungreased 18" × 26" baking sheets, about 2" apart. Bake for 12 minutes or until you see the edges of the cookies start to brown.

7. Once done, remove from oven, let cookies stand 2 minutes, then serve.

Molasses Cookies Dipped in White Chocolate

These are one of my all-time favorite cookies. I was introduced to these cookies by my mother-in-law Dodie Bell years ago. She would make sure to come to all our kids' sports games with her Molasses Cookies. She would walk up the stadium seats and hand out her cookies to anyone who wanted one, even complete strangers. Good thing she made dozens and dozens and dozens of them to share. This sweet woman is the one who introduced over-the-top baking to me. There is nothing a cookie from Grandma Dodie can't fix.

Prep Time: 30 minutes
Cook Time: 12 minutes per batch
Yields: 36 cookies

Ingredients:

¾ cup salted butter, softened
¾ cup shortening
2 cups packed light brown sugar
½ cup molasses
2 large eggs, slightly beaten
4 cups all-purpose flour
4 teaspoons baking soda
4 teaspoons ground ginger
2 teaspoons plus 1 tablespoon ground cinnamon, divided
2 teaspoons ground cloves
½ teaspoon Himalayan salt
2 tablespoons white sugar
1 cup white chocolate chips
1 teaspoon coconut oil

Steps:

1. Preheat oven to 350°F.

2. In a large bowl, combine butter, shortening, and brown sugar. Mix with a hand mixer for 5 minutes. Add in molasses and eggs and continue mixing until light and fluffy, about 5 minutes. Set aside.

3. In a separate large bowl, whisk together flour, baking soda, ginger, 2 teaspoons cinnamon, cloves, and salt. Add dry ingredients to the cream mixture and mix thoroughly.

4. In a shallow medium bowl or pie plate, combine remaining 1 tablespoon cinnamon with white sugar. Roll dough into 2" balls and then coat with the sugar mixture. Place onto ungreased 18" × 26" baking sheets, about 2" apart. Bake for 12 minutes or until you see the cookies' edges start to brown. Once done, remove from oven and let cool 5 minutes on pan before cooling completely on counter.

5. In a microwave-safe glass bowl, add white chocolate chips and oil. Heat in microwave in increments of 30 seconds, mixing well, until chocolate is smooth and creamy.

6. Dip half of each of the cooled cookies into melted chocolate, and place on parchment paper until chocolate hardens. Serve.

Izzy's Gluten-Free Monster Cookies

Whenever Izzy makes these cookies, they never last long. When my boys are trying to "get in shape," they tell us gals not to bake. How can you tell a mom and sisters that love being in the kitchen that they have to stop baking? Well, these cookies are great because they are gluten-free and have lots of protein and good stuff in them, but with lots of yumminess too.

Prep Time: 30 minutes
Cook Time: 10 minutes per batch
Yields: 36 cookies

Ingredients:
½ cup salted butter, softened
½ cup shortening
1 cup packed light brown sugar
1 tablespoon pure vanilla extract
3 large eggs, room temperature
1½ cups creamy peanut butter
2½ cups old-fashioned oats
2 cups quick-cooking oats
2 teaspoons baking soda
1 teaspoon Himalayan salt
1 cup peanut butter chips
I cup mini semisweet chocolate chips
1 cup cinnamon chips
1 cup mini M&M's

Steps:

1. Preheat oven to 350°F.

2. In a large bowl, cream together butter and shortening for 5 minutes until light and fluffy.

3. Add brown sugar and continue mixing, then add vanilla, eggs, and peanut butter and mix again, about 5 minutes.

4. To the same bowl, add all oats, baking soda, and salt. Mix for 5 minutes until well blended.

5. Using a wooden spoon, fold in chips and M&M's.

6. Place heaping tablespoons of dough about 2" apart on ungreased 18" × 26" baking sheets and bake for 10 minutes or until you see the edges of the cookies start to brown.

7. When done, remove from oven and let cool for 10 minutes, then transfer to wire racks to cool. (Don't remove the cookies too soon or they will fall apart. Give them time to set up.) Serve.

Pumpkin Roll Cheesecake Cookies

These cookies are a perfect addition to the pumpkin-flavored "everything" you encounter when fall time hits. The first day of September, I'm getting out my pumpkin-scented candles and running to the store to grab the pumpkin-flavored creamers. Then I start making my pumpkin chocolate chip bread, pumpkin cinnamon rolls, and my Pumpkin Roll Cheesecake Cookies. I'm that person that the Internet makes memes about that is obsessed with everything pumpkin until November 30th. Yep! That's me!

Prep Time: 30 minutes
Cook Time: 10 minutes per batch
Yields: 72 cookies

Ingredients:

2 cups salted butter, softened

2 cups white sugar

2 cups packed light brown sugar

4 large eggs

1 tablespoon vanilla bean paste (or pure vanilla extract)

2 tablespoons pumpkin purée

6 cups all-purpose flour

2 teaspoons baking soda

1 teaspoon Himalayan salt

2 (3.4-ounce) boxes pumpkin instant pudding mix

1 tablespoon pumpkin pie spice

1 (12-ounce) bag pumpkin spice latte chips (or cinnamon chips)

1 (12-ounce) bag cheesecake chips

Steps:

1. Preheat oven to 350°F.

2. In a large bowl, cream together butter and sugars until smooth, about 5 minutes. Beat in eggs one at a time, then stir in vanilla and pumpkin purée.

3. In a separate large bowl, whisk together flour, baking soda, salt, pudding mix, and pumpkin pie spice. Add to cream mixture slowly while continuing to mix, until dry ingredients are completely added.

4. With a wooden spoon, fold in chips. Using a tablespoon, drop dough onto ungreased 18" × 26" baking sheets, about 2" apart.

5. Bake for 10 minutes or until you see the edges of the cookies start to brown. Let cookies set for 5 minutes, then remove from baking sheets and serve.

Nana's Famous Chocolate Chip Cookies

When my mom, Nana, came to visit, my kids couldn't wait for her to walk through the door because they knew she was bringing her cookies. They are so good that my husband, Luke, and my son Robert would ask for her to send them in the mail for their birthdays. That's how good they are! I begged my mom for years for the recipe, but she insisted that it was a "family secret." Finally, at Christmastime a few years ago she gave me the recipe as a gift, and now I am sharing this recipe with you, approved by Nana. These go great served warm with a glass of cold milk.

Prep Time: 30 minutes
Cook Time: 12 minutes per batch
Yields: 72 cookies

Ingredients:

1½ cups unsalted butter, softened

1⅓ cups shortening

1 cup packed light brown sugar

1 cup white sugar

4 large eggs, room temperature

2 teaspoons pure vanilla extract

2 teaspoons almond extract

6 cups all-purpose flour

2 teaspoons baking soda

2 teaspoons Himalayan salt

2 (3.4-ounce) boxes French vanilla instant pudding mix

2 cups semisweet chocolate chips

2 cups mini semisweet chocolate chips

2 cups chopped walnuts

Steps:

1. Preheat oven to 350°F.

2. In a large bowl, cream together butter and shortening, about 5 minutes. Add both sugars and continue mixing for 5 minutes until mixture is light and fluffy.

3. To the same bowl, add eggs, vanilla, and almond extract. Mix about 5 minutes and set aside.

4. In a separate bowl, combine flour, baking soda, salt, and pudding mix and whisk thoroughly. Add half of dry mixture to cream mixture and mix for 5 minutes, then repeat with rest of dry mixture.

5. With a wooden spoon, fold in chips and walnuts.

6. Using a heaping full tablespoon, drop dough onto ungreased 18" × 26" baking sheets, about 2" apart. Bake for 12 minutes or until you see the edges of the cookies start to brown. Remove from oven and let stand for 5 minutes, then serve.

Loaded Peanut Butter Chocolate Chip Cookies

I have been a peanut butter cookie fan since I was a little girl. I always looked forward to my mom making them for me. I was in charge of taking the fork and making the crisscross pattern on top. My mom was the "original" cookie queen, so when I make them for my kids and sit at the table watching them enjoy the warm cookies, it brings back so many memories of my mom making them for me and my siblings and how she would sit at the table asking us how school was while we gobbled them up.

Prep Time: 30 minutes
Cook Time: 12 minutes per batch
Yields: 72 cookies

Ingredients:

1⅓ cups salted butter, softened
1⅓ cups shortening
1 cup packed light brown sugar
1 cup white sugar
½ cup creamy peanut butter (not natural)
4 large eggs, room temperature
4 teaspoons vanilla bean paste
6 cups all-purpose flour
2 teaspoons baking soda
2 teaspoons Himalayan salt
2 (3.4-ounce) boxes butterscotch instant pudding mix
1 cup peanut butter chips
1 cup mini semisweet chocolate chips
1 cup milk chocolate chips
1 cup Butterfinger baking pieces
1 cup Reese's Pieces peanut butter candy

Steps:

1. Preheat oven to 350°F.

2. In a large bowl, cream together butter, shortening, and sugars, about 5 minutes. Add peanut butter, eggs, and vanilla. Beat on medium speed for 5 minutes. Set aside.

3. In a separate large bowl, whisk together flour, baking soda, salt, and pudding mix. Slowly add flour mixture to the peanut butter mixture and mix for 5 minutes or until light and fluffy. Fold in all the chips and candy pieces.

4. Using a tablespoon, drop dough onto ungreased 18" × 26" baking sheets, about 2" apart. Bake for 12 minutes or until you see the edges of the cookies start to brown.

5. Once done, remove from oven and let stand for 5 minutes. Remove from sheet and serve.

Cast Iron Chocolate Chip–Stuffed Brownies

When I was growing up, my dad would make everything in cast iron pans. It didn't matter what it was; he was a terrific cook. It took me years to get comfortable making dinner with cast iron pans, never mind baking with them. But after embracing cast iron cooking, I decided to try my hand at baking, so I went online and bought some cast iron pie pans, baking sheets, baking pans, and brownie pans. I couldn't wait to use them, and my first thought was brownies— but with a twist! And so, I created my stuffed brownies with chocolate chip cookie dough. They are *amazing*!

Prep Time: 1 hour

Cook Time: 50 minutes

Yields: 14 servings

Ingredients:

1½ cups white sugar

1 cup salted butter

¼ cup water

3 cups milk chocolate chips, divided

2 teaspoons vanilla bean paste

4 large eggs, room temperature

1½ cups all-purpose flour

1 teaspoon baking soda

½ teaspoon Himalayan salt

1 batch Nana's Famous Chocolate Chip Cookies (walnuts omitted), unbaked (see recipe in this chapter)

Steps:

1. Preheat oven to 350°F.

2. In a large saucepan, combine sugar, butter, and water. Cook over medium heat until mixture comes to a boil, around 3–4 minutes making sure to stir constantly.

3. Remove from heat and add 2 cups chocolate chips and vanilla paste. Mix until smooth, then add eggs, one at a time, mixing between each one.

4. In a large bowl, whisk together flour, baking soda, and salt. Add to chocolate mixture along with remaining 1 cup chocolate chips. Continue stirring until flour mixture is well blended.

5. Pour into a greased 17" round cast iron pan. Drop cookie dough throughout brownie batter using a small scooper.

6. Bake for 40 minutes or until a toothpick inserted into the center comes out clean. Once done, let stand until cooled and then cut into squares and serve.

Robert's Favorite No-Bake Cookies

This is the one cookie that I struggle with. If you make them right, they are amazing; if not, they come out crumbly and dry. When you make these no-bake cookies you have to have all your ingredients measured out and ready to go because you can lose these cookies super-fast. They need the exact amount of cooking time, and you have to make sure all your attention is given to these cookies. So before you begin, make sure you can have at least 20 minutes all to yourself to be successful with these cookies.

Prep Time: 20 minutes
Cook Time: 25 minutes
Yields: 36 cookies

Ingredients:
½ cup salted butter
2 cups white sugar
½ cup cold whole milk
¼ cup unsweetened cocoa powder
½ cup creamy peanut butter
1 teaspoon pure vanilla extract
3 cups quick-cooking oats

Steps:

1. In a large saucepot, combine butter, sugar, milk, and cocoa. Cook over medium heat, stirring often until butter is melted and sugar is dissolved, about 5–10 minutes.

2. Once mixture starts to bubble and it continues to bubble while stirring constantly, set a timer for exactly 1 minute and continue stirring.

3. When timer is done, immediately remove pot from heat and stir in peanut butter and vanilla.

4. Fold in oats until blended and then immediately, using a scooper, place each cookie onto parchment paper and let set for 15 minutes until cookies set up and are completely cooled. Serve.

Deep-Fried Oreos

When Noah and I make our big breakfast for our family, he likes to be in charge of making pancakes and waffles—he even came up with a delicious and super-easy waffle recipe. I was completely impressed. The batter was nice and smooth, so I asked him if we could try making deep-fried Oreos using his recipe. Well, he didn't even hesitate because he loves Oreos. I kinda think we may have eaten more than were actually fried, which is okay with me. These turn out great, and are so easy to make.

Prep Time: 15 minutes
Cook Time: 4 minutes per Oreo
Yields: 24 Oreos

Ingredients:

4 cups avocado oil

2 cups all-purpose flour

2 tablespoons white sugar

4 teaspoons baking powder

$\frac{1}{2}$ teaspoon Himalayan salt

2 large eggs, room temperature

1 cup whole milk

1 cup heavy cream

$\frac{1}{4}$ cup salted butter, melted

1 (14.02-ounce) package Double Stuf Oreos

Steps:

1. In a medium saucepan, heat oil over medium heat.

2. In a large bowl, combine flour, sugar, baking powder, and salt and whisk together.

3. Add eggs, milk, cream, and butter. Mix together and set aside.

4. Check oil temperature with the wooden spoon test: Place spoon into oil and if small bubbles form along spoon, oil is ready to go.

5. Dip Oreos one at a time into batter, then into oil. When batter turns brown (about 2 minutes), flip Oreo over in oil to fry the other side. When both sides are browned, remove from oil and place on a plate lined with a paper towel. Repeat for remaining Oreos. Serve.

CHAPTER 9

Italian-Themed Recipes

~ ✳ ~

The three boys were neighbors before they moved in, and Brendon *used to knock on the door every time Mom made spaghetti to ask to eat dinner with the family.*

The boys lived next door to us in the rental and loved playing with our kids. Brendon would knock on the door every day asking if they could come out to play, and then he'd ask what was for dinner. The very first time he asked what I'd made for dinner was a Friday, and so I told him on Fridays we always eat spaghetti and meatballs. Well, according to this sweet eight-year-old boy, that was his very favorite dinner of all time. I started setting a place for him, and I found out shortly after that he would eat at home with his big brother Robert and his dad, then run over to our house and eat with us. He was especially excited for Friday nights when I made "his favorite meal of all time."

Brendon was so funny and was always telling Mr. Bell his new jokes that he had practiced and would come over to tell us; little did I know in the next few months he would move into our home with his big brother Robert. They moved into our home in October shortly after their dad passed, and it was a very sad time for all of us. Brendon was younger so he didn't understand it all, but I knew in my heart that these sweet boys were meant to be in our home. I think coming into a home with lots of kids and having the farm animals really helped them heal, and knowing they had so many people that loved them and loved their dad also helped. It's amazing how God works and brings different people into your life for a purpose. I truly believe that He knew what was going to happen to their dad and placed them into our lives to prepare us all for what was to come.

I truly can't imagine my life without Brendon in it. From day one he has been the funniest person around and seems to always know when you're struggling and will try to make you laugh and give you the biggest hug ever. Honestly, he brings the biggest smile to my face just by walking into the kitchen. All my kids know where to find me; when they come into the house, they walk straight into the kitchen. However, Brendon walks into the kitchen very different from his siblings: He will come in dancing, impersonating a famous person, or wearing the craziest outfit ever, and I love it!

Brendon was the first child to come into our home and not be a picky eater; he looked forward to dinnertime and couldn't wait to see what I'd made. He was the one who helped me set up the huge dining room table to get it ready for dinner and wanted to bring the actual meal in with everyone sitting around the table and place it right into the middle, then let the family know what I'd cooked. I truly think that what he enjoyed more than the actual dinner was sitting around our big dining room table and just talking with the entire family about how things are going. He really needed that closeness and bonding. I think he wanted that laughter and joy more than food.

Brendon is my outgoing child; he isn't one to keep his emotions hidden. He was a young boy when his dad passed away, and I reassured him that it was okay to be upset because he loved his father. His way of coping and dealing with loss was to make others laugh to bring happiness and joy. He took a tragedy in his life and created something beautiful to help others feel better. What bravery it takes for an eight-year-old boy who just lost one of the most important people in his life to use that experience to help others feel better when they are sad and hurt.

This chapter is dedicated to Brendon because over ten years ago it all started with a knock on the door for Friday night spaghetti and meatballs. When the boys moved in, Brendon wanted to not only help me set the table, but also to cook. He would always request lasagna, stuffed shells, spaghetti and meatballs, manicotti, and pretty much anything that was Italian. Instead of making this for him, I asked if he would like to help me. Brendon would do whatever he could to spend extra time with me alone, without his seven siblings. He really needed that one-on-one time with me in the kitchen and with Dad at the shop. I think out of all my children, he liked being with me in the kitchen the most. We had the best times because it wasn't only cooking homemade lasagna together but turning on the radio and dancing up a storm. That's what's great about our kitchen: It's not just for cooking but for talking, laughing, dancing, and for healing and wiping away tears. I'll tell you what—Brendon's Stuffed Manicotti can cure the saddest heart with just one bite! 🌹

Brendon's Stuffed Manicotti

Brendon could eat spaghetti morning, noon, and night. One of the first meals he made was Stuffed Manicotti, and it turned out great. The one thing about cooking Italian recipes is they are originally made for big families, like really big families, and so it fits our family. If you are trying to cook on a budget, pasta dishes are the perfect meals that not only are budget friendly but also can feed a crowd of people all at one sitting.

Prep Time: 30 minutes
Cook Time: 1 hour
Yields: 10 servings

Ingredients:

1 pound 90/10 lean ground beef

1 pound ground pork sausage

1 tablespoon minced fresh garlic

1 tablespoon dried Italian seasoning

1 (16-ounce) container ricotta cheese

2 tablespoons dried parsley

1 large egg

4 cups shredded Parmesan cheese, divided

2 (23.5-ounce) jars spaghetti sauce

2 (8-ounce) boxes manicotti shells, cooked

Steps:

1. Preheat oven to 375°F.

2. In a large saucepan over medium heat, combine beef, sausage, garlic, and Italian seasoning. Mix and cook for 15 minutes or until cooked through, stirring occasionally. Set aside.

3. In a medium bowl, combine ricotta, parsley, egg, and 2 cups Parmesan. Stir together and add half of the meat mixture. Stir again. Fill a large zip-top bag with the cheese/meat mixture and cut off one corner. Set aside.

4. Layer a greased 10" × 15" casserole dish with 1 jar spaghetti sauce. Next, layer with half of remaining meat mixture.

5. Fill each manicotti shell with cheese/meat mixture by squeezing mixture from bag into each shell. Place filled manicotti in the dish, setting each one side by side until the dish is filled.

6. Layer with remaining jar of sauce and the rest of meat mixture.

7. Top with remaining 2 cups Parmesan and bake for 45 minutes. Serve.

Homemade Spaghetti *and* Meatballs

When my kids were little, I made spaghetti and meatballs every single week but not homemade because as a busy mom to eight children ten and under I had to hurry and make dinner. Once my children grew up, they began to appreciate my home-cooked meals more and realize how much work it took to make dinner every single day for ten people. That's also when I had more time to make "from scratch" meals and take my time paying more attention to detail.

Prep Time: 45 minutes
Cook Time: 2 hours and **35** minutes
Yields: 10 servings

Sauce Ingredients:
1 large yellow onion, peeled and chopped
2 tablespoons olive oil
2 tablespoons minced fresh garlic
2 (29-ounce) cans tomato sauce
1 (28-ounce) can crushed tomatoes
2 (12-ounce) cans tomato paste
2 tablespoons dried minced onion
2 tablespoons dried Italian seasoning
2 tablespoons garlic powder
2 bay leaves
4 tablespoons dried parsley
1/2 teaspoon crushed red pepper flakes

Meatball Ingredients:
3 pounds 90/10 lean ground beef
3 large eggs
1 tablespoon garlic salt
3 tablespoons dried minced onion
2 tablespoons dried Italian seasoning
2 tablespoons garlic powder
1/4 cup quick-cooking oats
2 cups shredded Italian cheese mix

Additional Ingredients:
1 (16-ounce) box spaghetti, cooked

Steps:

1. **Make the Sauce:** In a large stockpot, combine onion, oil, and garlic. Cook over medium heat for 10 minutes, stirring occasionally. Then add the rest of the Sauce ingredients. Stir, reduce heat to low, and simmer for 2 hours, making sure to stir often.

2. Preheat oven to 400°F.

3. **Make the Meatballs:** In a large mixing bowl, combine all Meatball ingredients and form mixture into 2" balls. Place onto greased 18" × 26" baking sheets. Bake 15 minutes or until cooked through.

4. Once cooked through, place meatballs into spaghetti sauce and simmer for an additional 20 minutes, and then serve over spaghetti.

Million Dollar Spaghetti Pie

My mom came to visit and insisted on making dinner to give me a break from the kitchen. I had never heard about Million Dollar Spaghetti Pie until my mom made it for us. It is so amazing! Adding the cream cheese mixed with sour cream brings traditional spaghetti to a whole other level. I absolutely couldn't eat enough of it; it was so creamy and delicious. After she left, I had to make it again, but I made sure to double the recipe because I knew my kids were going to devour it. Thanks, Mom, for sharing it with me!

Prep Time: 30 minutes
Cook Time: 55 minutes
Yields: 10 servings

Ingredients:

2 pounds 90/10 lean ground beef

1 pound ground pork

1 large yellow onion, peeled and chopped

2 tablespoons minced fresh garlic

1 teaspoon ground black pepper

1 teaspoon Himalayan salt

1 (28-ounce) can crushed tomatoes

1 (67-ounce) jar spaghetti sauce

2 tablespoons dried Italian seasoning

2 (8-ounce) packages cream cheese, softened

1½ cups sour cream

1 (8-ounce) container ricotta cheese

1 tablespoon dried parsley

2 large eggs

2 cups shredded mozzarella cheese

1 (12-ounce) box spaghetti, cooked according to package directions

4 cups shredded Parmesan cheese

Steps:

1. Preheat oven to 375°F.

2. In a large stockpot over medium-high heat, combine beef, pork, onion, garlic, pepper, and salt. Stir together and cook for 15 minutes or until cooked through, stirring occasionally.

3. Drain grease and then add tomatoes, spaghetti sauce, and Italian seasoning to meat mixture. Stir together and set aside.

4. In a large bowl, combine cream cheese, sour cream, ricotta, parsley, eggs, and mozzarella. Stir together and set aside.

5. Add the spaghetti to the meat mixture and mix together. Fold in cheese mixture and then pour into an ungreased 10" × 15" casserole dish.

6. Bake for 40 minutes. Then remove from oven and sprinkle with Parmesan. Let stand for 10 minutes and serve.

Izzy's Stuffed Shells *with* Cheesy Garlic Bread

Here is another wonderful recipe from my daughter Izzy. Even when she was little, she was so comfortable in the kitchen. She walks in and takes charge of the kitchen, and you can see she is on a mission. She doesn't need advice on what seasonings to use with each dish. Just when I think her specialty is Mexican-inspired meals, she makes these stuffed shells that will blow your socks off, and of course, in true Izzy fashion, she makes it look so professional. If you don't have a piping bag for the filling, you can use a zip-top plastic bag with one corner cut off.

Prep Time: 35 minutes
Cook Time: 55 minutes
Yields: 10 servings

Ingredients:

1 pound 90/10 lean ground beef

1 pound ground pork sausage

1 tablespoon dried oregano

1/2 tablespoon dried basil

1 tablespoon minced fresh garlic

1/4 teaspoon crushed red pepper flakes

1 (24-ounce) jar spaghetti sauce

1 (8-ounce) container ricotta cheese

1 tablespoon garlic powder

4 tablespoons dried parsley, divided

1 teaspoon ground black pepper

1 teaspoon Himalayan salt

4 cups shredded Italian cheese mix

1 large egg

2 (24-ounce) boxes jumbo shells, cooked and dried on a paper towel

2 (13.5-ounce) frozen packages garlic bread

2 cups zesty Italian dressing

1 cup shredded mozzarella cheese

2 cups shredded Parmesan cheese

2 tablespoons garlic salt

Steps:

1. In an 8-quart stockpot over medium heat, combine beef, pork, oregano, basil, minced garlic, and red pepper flakes and cook for 15 minutes or until cooked through, stirring occasionally. Drain grease from the pot and reduce heat to low. Add sauce and simmer for 10 minutes, stirring a few times. Remove and set aside.

2. In a large mixing bowl, add ricotta, garlic powder, 2 tablespoons parsley, black pepper, salt, Italian cheese, and egg. Mix well, then fill a piping bag with the mixture and set aside.

3. Preheat oven to 375°F.

4. Layer an ungreased 10" × 15" casserole dish with 2 cups meat sauce and spread out evenly.

continued

continued

5. Using the piping bag, fill shells with cheese mixture. Then lay side by side in casserole on top of meat sauce.

6. Once shells are all filled, top with remainder of cheese mixture and then remainder of meat sauce. Bake for 30 minutes.

7. Once shells are in the oven, prepare garlic bread: Lay garlic bread on ungreased 18" × 26" baking sheets. Brush with Italian dressing and then top with mozzarella and Parmesan. Sprinkle with garlic salt and remaining 2 tablespoons parsley. Bake for 15 minutes. Serve.

Baked Chicken Parmesan

This recipe came about when I had just bought my first set of cast iron deep-dish baking pans and wanted to make the perfect dinner to show them off to my family. I had used my skillets to cook many times, but using baking pans was another challenge—one that I was ready for. I decided to make a baked chicken dish, and with my family's love for Italian dishes, I thought Baked Chicken Parmesan would be the perfect dinner. The chicken is so crispy and even better served with spaghetti.

Prep Time: 40 minutes
Cook Time: 35 minutes
Yields: 14 servings

Ingredients:

2 cups all-purpose flour
2 tablespoons heavy cream
9 large eggs
4 cups bread crumbs
1 cup shredded Parmesan cheese
2 tablespoons onion powder
½ tablespoon garlic salt
½ tablespoon ground white pepper
2 tablespoons dried Italian seasoning
14 (6-ounce) boneless, skinless chicken breasts
2 (24-ounce) jars three-cheese spaghetti sauce
4 cups shredded Italian cheese mix
2 (16-ounce) boxes spaghetti, cooked

Steps:

1. Preheat oven to 425°F.

2. Grab three glass pie plates or shallow medium bowls. In the first pie plate, add flour. In the second pie plate, combine cream and eggs and then beat lightly. In the third pie plate, combine bread crumbs, Parmesan, onion powder, garlic salt, pepper, and Italian seasoning. Mix and set aside.

3. Lightly coat each chicken breast with flour, then egg mixture, then bread crumb mixture, making sure to coat both sides. Place coated chicken into 2 (9" × 13") cast iron baking dishes.

4. Once all chicken has been coated, cover with sauce and cook for 20 minutes.

5. Remove from oven and sprinkle with Italian cheese. Place back into the oven for an additional 15 minutes. Serve over spaghetti.

Cast Iron Lasagna

My boys love lasagna, but I actually didn't start making it until the kids were older. I had tried a couple times and just couldn't figure it out. Either it came out too watery or so thick you couldn't even swallow it. So, I just gave up trying, and the only time my kids got to eat lasagna for dinner was when Grandma Dodie came to visit. Upon my boys' persistent begging for lasagna, I did my homework and searched out different recipes to see where I was going wrong. I finally figured it out and created my own version of lasagna and it was a hit.

Prep Time: 30 minutes
Cook Time: 1 hour and **10** minutes
Yields: 10 servings

Ingredients:

4 pounds 90/10 lean ground beef
1 large yellow onion, peeled and chopped
2 tablespoons minced fresh garlic
2 tablespoons dried minced onion
1 tablespoon garlic powder
2 tablespoons dried Italian seasoning
1 teaspoon crushed red pepper flakes
2 (24-ounce) jars spaghetti sauce
3 (14.5-ounce) cans fire-roasted tomatoes
1 (12-ounce) can tomato paste
1 (16-ounce) bag shredded Italian cheese mix
1 (16-ounce) container ricotta cheese
1 (8-ounce) package cream cheese
2 large eggs
1 tablespoon dried oregano
½ tablespoon garlic salt
1 teaspoon ground white pepper
2 (12-ounce) boxes oven-ready lasagna noodles
2 cups shredded medium Cheddar cheese

Steps:

1. Preheat oven to 375°F.

2. In a large saucepot over medium heat, combine beef, chopped onion, garlic, minced onion, garlic powder, Italian seasoning, and red pepper flakes. Cook for 15 minutes or until meat is cooked through, stirring occasionally. Remove from heat and add sauce, tomatoes, and paste. Mix and set aside.

3. In a medium bowl, combine Italian cheese, ricotta, cream cheese, eggs, oregano, garlic salt, and white pepper. Mix well and set aside.

4. Layer a 17" round cast iron pan with 2 cups meat sauce. Next, layer with noodles, a third of remaining meat sauce, noodles, and half of cheese mixture. Repeat layers and then end with noodles and remaining third meat sauce, then sprinkle with Cheddar.

5. Bake for 55 minutes and serve.

Creamy Chicken Pasta Primavera

The neat thing about making pasta dishes is all the different pasta shapes you can buy. Even though a majority of them are similar, I feel like each type of pasta brings something new to the character of the dish. There are certain dishes that I actually recognize by the type of pasta used, including this dish. I even get excited when I have to restock my pasta selection in the pantry because I love scanning the pasta shapes and looking for ones I have never seen or used before. Yes, I do get excited to go grocery shopping!

Prep Time: 30 minutes
Cook Time: 30 minutes
Yields: 12 servings

Ingredients:

4 pounds boneless, skinless chicken breasts, cut into slices

1 tablespoon garlic salt

$\frac{1}{2}$ tablespoon ground white pepper

2 tablespoons minced fresh garlic

1 (8-ounce) jar sun-dried tomatoes, drained (oil reserved) and chopped

$\frac{1}{2}$ cup salted butter

2 tablespoons dried Italian seasoning

1 medium red bell pepper, seeded and sliced

1 medium yellow bell pepper, seeded and sliced

1 (10-ounce) bag shredded carrots

2 medium zucchini, sliced into half moons

2 cups frozen peas

$\frac{1}{2}$ cup white cooking wine

2 cups heavy cream

1 (8-ounce) block cream cheese, cut into cubes

4 cups shredded Parmesan cheese, divided

2 (16-ounce) boxes penne pasta, cooked according to package directions

Steps:

1. In a 17" round cast iron pan, combine chicken, garlic salt, white pepper, minced garlic, and sun-dried tomatoes plus their oil. Cook over medium heat for 5 minutes, stirring occasionally.

2. Add butter, Italian seasoning, bell peppers, carrots, zucchini, and peas. Continue cooking and stirring occasionally for 10 minutes.

3. Stir in wine, heavy cream, and cream cheese. Cook for an additional 10 minutes, making sure to stir often until cheese has melted.

4. Add 2 cups Parmesan and penne, then reduce heat to low and simmer for 5 minutes.

5. Serve dish with remaining 2 cups Parmesan sprinkled on top.

Hailey's Vegetarian Lasagna

We don't normally make dinners that are vegetarian, but Hailey was up for the challenge. I was pretty impressed that she wanted to tackle this task. She wanted to try her hand at making a lasagna that was just plant based or veggies only. It turned out to be similar to a traditional lasagna but extra veggies added. Honestly, I think the best part of lasagna is that creamy cheese layer—the more cheese the better. She used plant-based beef, and you couldn't even tell the difference, it's that delicious.

Prep Time: 45 minutes
Cook Time: 1 hour and **25** minutes
Yields: 12 servings

Ingredients:

2 (13.7-ounce) packages frozen plant-based ground beef
1 large yellow onion, peeled and chopped
1 large red bell pepper, seeded and chopped
4 cups peeled and chopped carrots
2 tablespoons dried minced onion
2 tablespoons dried basil
1 tablespoon dried Italian seasoning
1 teaspoon garlic salt
1 teaspoon ground black pepper
2 tablespoons minced fresh garlic
2 (15-ounce) cans fire-roasted tomatoes
1 (28-ounce) can crushed tomatoes
2 (29-ounce) cans tomato purée
2 (24-ounce) jars spaghetti sauce
1 (8-ounce) jar sun-dried tomatoes, drained and chopped
2 cups chopped fresh spinach leaves
1/2 cup water
2 tablespoons red wine vinegar
2 tablespoons white sugar
4 tablespoons dried parsley, divided
1 tablespoon garlic powder
2 cups shredded Italian cheese mix
1 large egg
1 (8-ounce) container ricotta cheese
2 (9-ounce) boxes oven-ready lasagna noodles
6 cups shredded mozzarella cheese

Steps:

1. In an 8-quart stockpot over medium heat, combine plant-based beef, chopped onion, bell pepper, carrots, minced onion, basil, Italian seasoning, garlic salt, pepper, and minced garlic. Stir and cook for 15 minutes.

2. Add fire-roasted tomatoes, crushed tomatoes, tomato purée, spaghetti sauce, sun-dried tomatoes, and spinach. Stir and cook for another 15 minutes.

continued

continued

3. Reduce heat to low. Add water, vinegar, sugar, 2 table-spoons parsley, and garlic powder. Stir again and simmer for 10 minutes. Remove from heat and set aside.

4. In a large bowl, add Italian cheese, egg, ricotta, and remaining 2 tablespoons parsley. Stir together and set aside.

5. Preheat oven to 400°F.

6. Layer bottom of a 10" × 15" casserole dish with 1 cup "meat" sauce, spreading out evenly. Next, layer with noodles, half of cheese mixture, and 2 cups mozzarella.

7. Repeat layers and finish with noodles, rest of "meat" sauce, then mozzarella.

8. Bake for 45 minutes. Serve.

Izzy's Shrimp Fettuccine *with* Antipasto Salad

My husband loves dinners with any kind of seafood. Izzy makes a terrific pasta and surprised Dad with this shrimp fettuccine. My husband works so hard for our family, and she wanted to treat him to a nice homemade seafood dinner after he got home from working all day. When my husband walks into the house after a long day of work and sees one of the kids in the kitchen cooking, it makes his heart happy.

Prep Time: 30 minutes
Cook Time: 35 minutes
Yields: 10 servings

Shrimp Fettuccine Ingredients:

1 cup salted butter

2 medium green bell peppers, seeded and chopped

1 cup all-purpose flour

2 tablespoons minced fresh garlic

1 teaspoon Himalayan salt

1 teaspoon ground black pepper

2 cups heavy cream

2 cups whole milk

2 teaspoons ground nutmeg

1 (24-ounce) bag frozen, raw, peeled, and deveined large shrimp, tails off

1 (16-ounce) box fettuccine pasta, cooked according to package directions

2 medium tomatoes, diced

Homemade Italian Dressing Ingredients:

2 cups olive oil

$1/2$ cup red wine vinegar

2 tablespoons dried Italian seasoning

1 teaspoon garlic salt

$1 1/2$ teaspoons garlic powder

$1/4$ teaspoon crushed red pepper flakes

2 teaspoons white sugar

$1/4$ cup shredded Parmesan cheese

Antipasto Salad Ingredients:

6 cups chopped romaine lettuce

2 (6-ounce) packages thin-sliced salami lunch meat

2 (4-ounce) packages large, thin-sliced pepperoni

1 (11-ounce) package block provolone cheese, cut into slices

1 (11-ounce) package block mozzarella cheese, cut into slices

2 (6-ounce) containers feta cheese

2 cups grape tomatoes, sliced in half

1 (16-ounce) jar roasted red peppers, drained

1 (10-ounce) jar garlic-stuffed green olives, sliced into halves

1 (12-ounce) can pitted black olives, chopped

1 (14-ounce) can artichoke hearts, drained and chopped

continued

continued

Steps:

1. **Make the Shrimp Fettuccine:** In a 10-quart stockpot over medium heat, combine butter and bell peppers and cook for 5 minutes, stirring occasionally.

2. Add flour, minced garlic, salt, and black pepper. Whisk for 5 minutes until a paste forms, then continue to cook until bubbly, about 1 minute.

3. Slowly add cream while continuing to whisk, then add milk and nutmeg. Reduce heat to low and let simmer for 10 minutes to allow sauce to thicken, stirring occasionally.

4. Add shrimp, fettuccine, and tomatoes and continue to simmer over low heat for an additional 10 minutes, stirring as needed. Set aside.

5. **Make the Homemade Italian Dressing:** Combine all Homemade Italian Dressing ingredients in a medium jar and place the lid on top. Shake well and set aside.

6. **Make the Antipasto Salad:** Fill a large bowl with all the Antipasto Salad ingredients and toss with tongs. Drizzle Homemade Italian Dressing on top.

7. Serve the Shrimp Fettuccine with the fresh Antipasto Salad on the side.

Spaghetti *and* Meatball Sliders

This meal is like a meatball sub but on Hawaiian sweet rolls. I used a different meatball recipe than the one I use in my Homemade Spaghetti and Meatballs since this is a sandwich. I wanted to make sure that when you eat it, the meatballs will stay together to get the whole meatball slider experience. They are a great go-to if you're bored with the traditional "sandwich" for lunch. By brushing garlic butter onto the rolls, it's like eating a complete dinner in one bite.

Prep Time: 20 minutes
Cook Time: 40 minutes
Yields: 12 servings

Meatball Ingredients:

2 pounds 90/10 lean ground beef

1 pound ground pork

3 large eggs

2 tablespoons Worcestershire sauce

2 tablespoons minced fresh garlic

1 tablespoon Dijon mustard

1 tablespoon dried minced onion

1 tablespoon dried oregano

½ tablespoon Himalayan salt

½ tablespoon ground black pepper

2 cups shredded Parmesan cheese

Additional Ingredients:

1 (16-ounce) box spaghetti, cooked

1 (24-ounce) jar spaghetti sauce

3 (12-count) packages Hawaiian sweet rolls

1 cup salted butter, melted

½ tablespoon dried parsley

½ tablespoon garlic salt

8 cups shredded Italian cheese mix

Steps:

1. Preheat oven to 375°F.

2. In a large bowl, combine all Meatball ingredients and mix until everything is completely combined. Roll into 1" balls, place onto greased 18" × 26" baking sheets, and bake for 15 minutes or until cooked through.

3. In another large bowl, combine cooked spaghetti and sauce. Stir together and set aside.

4. Cut rolls in half horizontally and place tops and bottoms onto ungreased 18" × 26" baking sheets. In a small bowl, combine butter, parsley, and garlic salt. Brush inside of rolls with butter mixture and then bake them for 10 minutes.

5. Layer bottoms of rolls with half of Italian cheese, then meatballs, then spaghetti. Top with remaining half of Italian cheese and place tops on.

6. Brush leftover butter mixture over tops and return sliders to oven to bake for 15 minutes. Serve.

Chicken *and* Broccoli Tortellini

My husband and I like to go out for dinner on the weekends to a wonderful Italian restaurant. That is where I was first introduced to cheese tortellini. I couldn't get enough of it, and I knew that I had to check the grocery store to see if I could buy tortellini. To my surprise, they sell a lot of different kinds. I grabbed several bags and came straight home to see what I could make for my family that was way cheaper than the restaurant. This recipe was another hit for our family, and they even tolerated the broccoli!

Prep Time: 30 minutes
Cook Time: 50 minutes
Yields: 14 servings

Ingredients:

4 cups chopped fresh broccoli

3 (12-ounce) packages uncooked tortellini

8 cups water

1 cup salted butter, divided

4 pounds boneless, skinless chicken breasts, cut into 2" cubes

1 (10-ounce) bag shredded carrots

2 tablespoons minced fresh garlic

1 tablespoon garlic powder

1 tablespoon dried parsley

2 tablespoons dried minced onion

1 cup all-purpose flour

½ tablespoon garlic salt

½ tablespoon ground white pepper

2 teaspoons ground nutmeg

2 cups heavy cream

6 cups chicken stock (or broth)

2 cups shredded Italian cheese mix

4 cups shredded Parmesan cheese, plus more for serving

Steps:

1. In an 8-quart stockpot, add broccoli, tortellini, and water. Cook over medium heat for 20 minutes. Drain and return to pot. Set aside.

2. In a large skillet over medium heat, combine ½ cup butter, chicken, carrots, minced garlic, garlic powder, parsley, and minced onion. Sauté for 15 minutes. Transfer everything in skillet to the pot with tortellini.

3. Into the same skillet, add remaining ½ cup butter and continue cooking over medium heat for 5 minutes, then add flour, garlic salt, pepper, and nutmeg. Whisk for 3 minutes until a paste forms, then let simmer for 1 minute. Slowly add cream, continuing to whisk, then add stock.

4. Add both cheeses and stir until cheese melts, then pour sauce over chicken and tortellini mixture. Fold together with a wooden spoon and serve with Parmesan on top.

Chicken Carbonara

Whenever we go out to eat, I'm inspired to try to make the same dishes at home but with a "Mama Bell" tweak. My favorite Italian dishes have a white sauce, and you can add so many different ingredients to change up the taste. Make a cheese sauce, add bacon and noodles, and I'm sold! I like to challenge myself to try new techniques that I've never done before, like adding egg without scrambling it in the process. Being a chicken farmer, I know that there is nothing wrong with a perfect scrambled egg, but not for this recipe!

Prep Time: 30 minutes
Cook Time: 15 minutes
Yields: 12 servings

Ingredients:

2 (12-ounce) boxes linguine pasta, uncooked
4 large eggs
1 cup heavy cream
1 cup shredded Parmesan cheese
$\frac{1}{8}$ teaspoon crushed red pepper flakes
2 tablespoons dried Italian seasoning
1 pound bacon, cut into pieces
4 pounds boneless, skinless chicken breasts, cut into slices
2 tablespoons minced fresh garlic
1 tablespoon garlic salt
$\frac{1}{2}$ tablespoon ground white pepper
1 tablespoon dried parsley
2 cups shredded Italian cheese mix

Steps:

1. Bring a large stockpot of water to a boil and add linguine. Cook until al dente, then remove $\frac{1}{2}$ cup pasta water before straining pasta.

2. In a large bowl, combine eggs, cream, Parmesan, red pepper flakes, and Italian seasoning. Mix and set aside.

3. In a 17" round cast iron pan, add bacon and cook over medium heat for 10 minutes until fully cooked. Remove from the pan and place on a plate lined with a paper towel.

4. To the pan, add chicken, minced garlic, garlic salt, white pepper, and parsley. Sauté for 5 minutes over medium heat until just cooked through. Return bacon to the pan and add warm linguine. Toss together with tongs.

5. Remove pan from heat and let stand for 5 minutes before adding egg mixture. (This is to keep the eggs from being scrambled if pan is too hot.)

6. Pour egg mixture over pasta and chicken, then toss until fully coated. If needed, stir in $\frac{1}{2}$ cup pasta water until creamy.

7. Serve right away with Italian cheese sprinkled on top.

CHAPTER 10

Chili and Soup Recipes

~ ❋ ~

Noah *is the youngest of the three brothers and completed the family perfectly. At first, he was quiet and always asked to eat soup—it didn't matter what kind.*

Noah was the perfect person to complete our family of ten. I can't even begin to tell you how much I love this boy. He truly is the most compassionate and sweetest person I have ever met. He loves our family so much, and you can see it in his actions. He is the one that remembers everyone's birthdays and makes sure to get a present. He tries to help out wherever he can, and he pretty much takes care of me when Dad is working. I remember the very first day I met him. He had the biggest, most beautiful eyes I had ever seen, and they were so kind and caring.

Noah has always been my shy and quiet child, and when he was younger, he rarely said anything unless he was asking me if I could make him a grilled cheese sandwich so he could dip it into tomato soup. If he heard me say I was making soup, it didn't matter what kind of soup, he would immediately run to the bread drawer and grab the bread, then open up the huge fridge with his little hand and reach for the butter. Next, he'd grab a chair, put it next to the countertop, and open the silverware drawer to grab a butter knife or spoon (it didn't matter as long as it spread butter!). I would grab the cheese, and together we would get all the grilled cheeses cooking for the family. This is one of the main reasons we have to do mini grocery hauls—bread goes really fast in our house, especially during fall and winter when we make soup at least once a week.

When you have a big family, the youngest usually gets left to himself, but not in our home. Shortly after Noah moved in, Hailey came into our home, and she was so in love with Noah that she decided she would be the big sister and be in charge of him. She helped him pick out his clothes, made him breakfast and lunch, and pretty much took him wherever she went. They were very close growing up; plus, his other soon-to-be big sister Izzy was excited to have a friend her age to hang out and play together.

Noah came into our home when he was little, and he really didn't understand why he was in this new home. We kept our home open to his birth mom, and loving her like we loved the boys helped not only him to heal but also the older boys. As he got older, he had the support of our big family, including his brothers, and he was able to keep his mom in his life. It was very important for Luke and me to have our door open and to allow family members to still be a part of their children's lives, even after we adopted them, because we all need each other's support.

Noah has always been my "go-to guy." We have accomplished so much together. If I need something built or hauled somewhere, I know I can count on him. When he was thirteen years old, he built a pantry in my kitchen and a bench for my entryway. Our favorite thing is to grab a coffee (well, he gets hot cocoa) and go grocery shopping. Plus, he always has a recipe that he wants to try, so he brings his list and we grab what he needs. No matter where I am, Noah seems to be close, whether it's sitting at the kitchen counter watching me cook or standing next to me helping me get dinner on the table. When I look at him, it's hard to believe the young man he has grown into, because I still see that three-year-old boy with fluffy hair and big blue eyes looking at me.

The last chapter in our family cookbook is rightfully dedicated to my sweet Noah. He would slide a chair over the most to watch me cook. (Well, first he would ask for chocolate milk or hot cocoa, and then he would watch me make dinner!) He just watched quietly and at times asked me questions about cooking. He still today loves making soup, but chili is his all-time favorite. It makes me so happy watching him cook and run around the kitchen like me. I try so hard to be quiet and watch— if I give him cooking tips or suggestions, he looks at me with a smile and replies, "I know, Mom." Noah was the most perfect completion of our family. God sure knew what He was doing by bringing this sweet and kind boy into our lives. 🌹

Noah's Famous Venison Chili

Noah loves to fish and hunt. He enjoys being out in nature, plus he enjoys contributing to the family. I think he feels like he needs to be like Dad and take care of the family by helping provide food for dinnertime. Being the youngest of eight, he also tries really hard to make his siblings proud of him. There hasn't been a recipe yet that he has made with venison that I haven't liked, and I'm not the only one: This chili recipe won in our annual chili cook-off at church.

Prep Time: 35 minutes
Cook Time: 1 hour and **5** minutes
Yields: 12 servings

Ingredients:

1 cup salted butter

2 pounds ground venison

2 pounds lean venison steak, cut into 1" cubes

1 large yellow onion, peeled and chopped

2 tablespoons minced fresh garlic

2 tablespoons onion powder

1 tablespoon garlic salt

2 tablespoons chili powder

2 (14.5-ounce) cans garlic fire-roasted tomatoes

2 (29-ounce) cans tomato sauce

1 (28-ounce) can crushed tomatoes

1 (29-ounce) can pinto beans

1 (40-ounce) can chili beans

2 teaspoons crushed red pepper flakes

2 teaspoons smoked paprika

2 teaspoons ground cumin

2 cups frozen sweet corn

2 (9.25-ounce) bags chili cheese corn chips

6 cups shredded medium Cheddar cheese

4 cups sour cream

Steps:

1. In a 10-quart stockpot, combine butter, venison, chopped onion, minced garlic, onion powder, garlic salt, chili powder, and fire-roasted tomatoes. Cook over medium-low heat for 20 minutes, stirring occasionally. (If you cook venison too fast at higher temperatures it will get tough and chewy.)

2. Add tomato sauce, crushed tomatoes, beans, red pepper flakes, paprika, cumin, and corn. Cook over medium heat for 15 minutes, stirring a few times, then reduce the heat to low and continue cooking uncovered for 30 minutes, stirring as needed.

3. To serve, place a handful of corn chips in a bowl and top with chili. Then top chili with cheese and sour cream.

Italian Wedding Soup

This soup is super simple to make. I really love making this because of the little meatballs you add to it. During the winter, I'll wake up in the morning and start putting my ingredients together and let it simmer. There is nothing like watching the snow fall outside the window and smelling a nice pot of soup that will warm my family up when they get home from school and working outside.

Prep Time: 45 minutes
Cook Time: 1 hour and **30** minutes
Yields: 12 servings

Ingredients:

8 cups chicken broth

1 large yellow onion, peeled and diced

2 cups peeled and chopped carrots

2 tablespoons plus 1 teaspoon minced fresh garlic, divided

1 tablespoon plus 1 teaspoon dried parsley, divided

½ tablespoon plus 1 teaspoon salt, divided

½ tablespoon plus 1 teaspoon ground black pepper, divided

1 tablespoon plus 1 teaspoon dried oregano, divided

1 tablespoon dried Italian seasoning

1 pound ground pork

1 pound 90/10 lean ground beef

½ cup shredded Parmesan cheese

1 tablespoon onion powder

1 large egg

⅓ cup bread crumbs

4 tablespoons avocado oil

1 (16-ounce) box small shell pasta, uncooked

2 cups fresh spinach leaves

Steps:

1. In a 10-quart stockpot over low heat, add broth, diced onion, carrots, 2 tablespoons garlic, 1 tablespoon parsley, ½ tablespoon salt, ½ tablespoon pepper, 1 tablespoon oregano, and Italian seasoning. Simmer for 45 minutes, stirring occasionally.

2. In a large bowl, combine pork, beef, cheese, onion powder, egg, bread crumbs, and remaining 1 teaspoon each of garlic, parsley, salt, pepper, and oregano. Mix well and roll into 1½" balls.

3. Heat oil over medium heat in a large skillet and add meatballs. Cook for about 15 minutes, browning both sides.

4. Add meatballs to the stockpot along with pasta and spinach. Simmer over low heat for an additional 30 minutes, making sure pasta is cooked through. Serve.

Chicken Noodle Soup *with* Homemade Egg Noodles

This Chicken Noodle Soup with Homemade Egg Noodles is my daughter Izzy's favorite soup of all time. I make this quite a bit during the fall and winter months or if one of my kids isn't feeling too well. There is nothing like a bowl of chicken soup to help warm your insides up and make you feel better. When I went to visit my family, my sister-in-law taught me how to make these homemade egg noodles, and I couldn't believe how easy it was!

Prep Time: 45 minutes
Cook Time: 1 hour and **50** minutes
Yields: 10 servings

Ingredients:

5 quarts water

1 (5-pound) whole chicken, innards removed

2 tablespoons dried minced onion

2 tablespoons dried Italian seasoning

3 tablespoons dried parsley, divided

2 tablespoons minced fresh garlic, divided

1 cup all-purpose flour

$\frac{1}{2}$ teaspoon Himalayan salt

2 large eggs

$\frac{1}{2}$ cup salted butter

1 large white onion, peeled and diced

4 cups each of chopped celery and peeled and chopped carrots

1 tablespoon onion powder

$\frac{1}{2}$ tablespoon each of garlic salt and ground white pepper

Steps:

1. In a 19-quart stockpot over medium heat, add water, chicken, minced onion, Italian seasoning, 2 tablespoons parsley, and 1 tablespoon minced garlic. Cook for 1 hour until fully cooked.

2. In a medium bowl, whisk flour and salt together. Pour onto the countertop, make a well in the center, and crack eggs into the middle. With a fork, scramble the eggs lightly, slowly pulling in the flour until you have combined all the flour and it starts to form a ball. Then knead with both hands six to seven times. Wrap dough in plastic wrap and place in fridge for 30 minutes.

3. In a medium saucepan, add butter, diced onion, celery, and carrots. Cook over medium heat for 10 minutes, stirring occasionally. Add onion powder, garlic salt, pepper, and remaining 1 tablespoon each of parsley and minced garlic. Mix and cook for another 10 minutes, stirring a few times.

4. Remove chicken from the pot and pull meat off the bones, then return back to the pot. Add veggie mixture and let simmer for 15 minutes, stirring occasionally.

5. Remove dough from fridge and roll out thinly on a floured surface. Cut into $\frac{1}{2}$" strips. Separate and lay out onto cooling racks to dry for 10 minutes. Add noodles to soup and let simmer for another 15 minutes, then serve.

Dad's Everything but the Kitchen Sink Chili

I love that my family is comfortable in the kitchen. My husband doesn't cook too often because he is gone all day working hard for our family—and when he walks in the door, I want to have a nice meal for him to show how much I appreciate all he does for us. However, he is a great cook and I know that when I need a break, he will step up to the plate and make an amazing dinner to give me a night off. This chili recipe is great if you have leftovers or need to just throw something together fast.

Prep Time: 30 minutes
Cook Time: 1 hour and **25** minutes
Yields: 12 servings

Ingredients:

2 pounds 90/10 lean ground beef

2 pounds ground pork sausage

1 large yellow onion, peeled and diced

1 (14-ounce) package cheesy brats, chopped

2 tablespoons minced fresh garlic

2 tablespoons chili powder

1 (5-pound) bag Yukon Gold potatoes, cut into 1" cubes

2 cups frozen sweet corn

$\frac{1}{2}$ cup salted butter

1 tablespoon garlic salt

2 (29-ounce) cans tomato sauce

1 (27-ounce) can kidney beans

1 (27-ounce) can red beans

Steps:

1. In a large skillet over medium heat, combine beef, sausage, and onion and cook for 15 minutes, stirring occasionally. Add brats, minced garlic, and chili powder, and continue to cook for another 10 minutes.

2. With a slotted spoon, transfer meat mixture to an 8-quart Dutch oven, reserving the drippings in the pan.

3. To the pan with drippings, add potatoes, corn, butter, and garlic salt. Cook over medium heat for 20 minutes, stirring frequently, then add contents of the pan to the Dutch oven, including the drippings.

4. Add tomato sauce and beans. Cook over low heat for 40 minutes, stirring often. Serve.

Homemade Potato *and* Ham Soup

When I was growing up, my dad made potato soup often. He added bacon, chives, and Cheddar cheese. It was amazing. We knew when Dad was going to make his yummy soup because he would take everything out and prep it so when he got home from work the next day, he could just start cooking. My sisters and I would run into the kitchen after school, grab the white bread, throw it in the toaster, then spread a ton of butter on top and dip it into our soup. It was soooo good.

Prep Time: 30 minutes
Cook Time: 40 minutes
Yields: 14 servings

Ingredients:
1/2 cup salted butter
4 cups chopped celery
1 bunch green onions, ends trimmed, chopped
4 cups peeled and chopped carrots
1 tablespoon minced fresh garlic
8 1/2 cups chicken broth, divided
1 tablespoon dried parsley
1 tablespoon dried minced onion
1 tablespoon garlic powder
1 tablespoon ground white pepper
4 cups chopped deli smoked ham
1 (32-ounce) bag frozen shredded hash browns
2 cups fresh spinach leaves
1 ham bone
2 cups sour cream
1/2 tablespoon Himalayan salt
1/2 tablespoon ground black pepper
2 cups heavy cream
2 cups shredded medium Cheddar cheese

Steps:

1. In a 10-quart stockpot, melt butter over medium heat, then add celery, green onions, carrots, minced garlic, and 1/2 cup broth. Stir together and cook for 10 minutes.

2. Add parsley, minced onion, garlic powder, and white pepper. Simmer for another 10 minutes.

3. Add ham, hash browns, spinach, ham bone, sour cream, remaining 8 cups broth, salt, and black pepper. Stir together. Slowly add heavy cream and cheese, whisking while adding. Reduce heat to low and simmer for an additional 20 minutes, stirring occasionally. Serve.

Chicken *and* Dumpling Soup

Every summer when I was little, our family would get into our old station wagon and take the two-day trip to my grandmother's house. The two things I looked forward to were the candy dish by the front door and her wonderful chicken and dumpling soup that would be ready for us when we arrived. This recipe is the one thing that brings me the best memories of visiting my grandmother. Caving to much persistence, my mom shared her recipe with me—and while it might not be as good as my grandmother's, it's a close second.

Prep Time: 40 minutes
Cook Time: 2 hours and **20** minutes
Yields: 14 servings

Homemade Chicken Stock Ingredients:

1 (5-pound) whole chicken, innards removed
2½ quarts water
1 tablespoon dried basil
1 tablespoon dried thyme
2 tablespoons dried parsley
2 tablespoons minced fresh garlic
2 tablespoons dried minced onion
1 tablespoon dried bell pepper mix

Soup Ingredients:

1 cup salted butter
4 cups peeled and diced carrots
4 cups diced celery
1 medium yellow onion, peeled and diced
1 cup all-purpose flour
½ tablespoon ground white pepper
½ tablespoon Himalayan salt
4 cups whole milk
4 cups Homemade Chicken Stock (from this recipe)
2 (8-count) tubes refrigerated biscuits

Steps:

1. **Make the Homemade Chicken Stock:** In a 5-quart stockpot over medium heat, add Homemade Chicken Stock ingredients. Cook for 1 hour. Then reduce heat to low and simmer for 45 minutes.

2. Remove chicken and take meat off bones, then set meat aside. Strain stock into a large bowl.

3. **Make the Soup:** In a 10-quart stockpot, combine butter, carrots, celery, and onion. Cook over medium heat for 20 minutes, stirring occasionally. Sprinkle veggies with flour, pepper, and salt. Stir to coat veggies well. Reduce heat to low and simmer for 5 minutes. Then slowly, while stirring, add milk and then stock and simmer for an additional 5 minutes. Add chicken meat and stir to combine.

4. Cut each biscuit into four parts. Increase heat to medium-high. Once soup comes to a boil, drop in biscuit pieces. Stir well and reduce heat to medium. Cook for 5 minutes until biscuits are cooked through, then serve.

Broccoli Cheddar Soup

I sure love making a good soup. My daughter Hailey always asks me if I could make Broccoli Cheddar Soup, but I had never made it before. So, I did some searching and came up with this recipe. The best thing about this soup recipe is that it's so creamy and smooth. Be careful when making it because if your heat is too high when you add the Cheddar cheese you will separate the cheese and end up with broccoli and Cheddar chunk soup. Just sayin!!

Prep Time: 30 minutes
Cook Time: 45 minutes
Yields: 12 servings

Ingredients:

½ cup salted butter
1 cup all-purpose flour
1 tablespoon salt
1 tablespoon ground black pepper
2 cups heavy cream
2 cups whole milk
4 cups chicken broth
2 tablespoons paprika
2 tablespoons garlic powder
2 tablespoons minced fresh garlic
2 tablespoons dried minced onion
1 (8-ounce) package cream cheese, cubed
4 tablespoons sour cream
4 cups shredded medium Cheddar cheese
2 (10-ounce) bags shredded carrots
2 (12-ounce) bags shredded broccoli slaw

Steps:

1. In a 10-quart stockpot, combine butter, flour, salt, and pepper. Whisk over medium heat until a paste forms, about 2 minutes. Cook for 3 more minutes; it should be bubbling.

2. While whisking constantly, slowly add heavy cream, then milk, and lastly broth. Simmer over medium heat for 10 minutes, whisking.

3. Add paprika, garlic powder, minced garlic, and minced onion. Mix well, reduce heat to low, and then add cream cheese, sour cream, and Cheddar. Cook over low heat for 15 minutes, making sure to stir often.

4. Add carrots and broccoli slaw and continue to simmer for another 15 minutes. Serve.

White Chicken Chili

My mom shared this recipe with me years ago, but for some reason I always try to remember it without writing the recipe down. So every time I decide to make it, I have to give her a call and ask for her recipe all over again. It just gives me an excuse to grab a cup of coffee, call my mom, and visit. I think she got tired of me asking over and over, so she wrote it down on a recipe card for me. But for the life of me I can't seem to find it! Oh well, more coffee and mom time coming soon.

Prep Time: 40 minutes
Cook Time: 1 hour and **10** minutes
Yields: 12 servings

Ingredients:

3 pounds boneless, skinless chicken breasts

2 tablespoons garlic powder

1 tablespoon garlic salt

4 tablespoons ground cumin

3 tablespoons chili powder

1 (4-ounce) can chopped green chilies

1/2 cup salted butter

1 large yellow onion, peeled and chopped

4 cups chopped celery

4 cups peeled and chopped carrots

2 tablespoons dried oregano

2 tablespoons dried parsley

2 tablespoons dried minced onion

2 tablespoons minced fresh garlic

4 cups chicken broth

1 (48-ounce) jar Randall's mixed assorted white beans

2 cups heavy cream

2 cups sour cream

1 (8-ounce) block cream cheese, cubed

Steps:

1. In a large saucepot, combine chicken, garlic powder, garlic salt, cumin, chili powder, and green chilies. Cook over medium heat for 20 minutes, stirring occasionally.

2. In an 8-quart stockpot, melt butter and then add chopped onion, celery, and carrots. Cook over medium heat for 10 minutes, stirring occasionally, then add oregano, parsley, minced onion, and minced garlic. Stir and continue cooking for another 10 minutes.

3. To the 8-quart pot, add chicken mixture, broth, and beans. Reduce heat to low and simmer for 15 minutes, stirring occasionally.

4. While stirring, add heavy cream, sour cream, and cream cheese. Continue cooking on low heat for 15 minutes until cheese is melted and soup is nice and creamy. Serve.

Creamy Chicken Tortellini Soup

Tortellini is one of my favorite pastas because it's filled with meat or cheese. I use it as a pasta meal often but wasn't sure if it would work as a yummy soup too. Well, it was just as good in a soup! I get asked a lot to name my favorite dish to make, and after thinking about it, I am gonna say soup. Any kind of soup. Soup is like my casseroles, a one dish wonder but in liquid form!

Prep Time: 40 minutes
Cook Time: 1 hour and **40** minutes
Yields: 14 servings

Homemade Chicken Stock Ingredients:

5 quarts water

4 pounds boneless, skinless chicken breasts

2 tablespoons each of dried parsley, dried minced onion, garlic powder, and dried Italian seasoning

½ tablespoon garlic salt

½ tablespoon ground black pepper

Soup Ingredients:

2 (12-ounce) packages uncooked tortellini

½ cup salted butter

1 cup all-purpose flour

1 tablespoon minced fresh garlic

1 teaspoon each of Himalayan salt and ground black pepper

2 cups heavy cream

1 (10-ounce) bag matchstick carrots

1 (8-ounce) block cream cheese

2 cups shredded Italian cheese mix

4 cups fresh spinach leaves

Steps:

1. **Make the Homemade Chicken Stock:** In a 10-quart stock-pot over medium heat, combine Homemade Chicken Stock ingredients. Cook for 15 minutes, then reduce heat to low and simmer for 30 minutes. When chicken is cooked through, transfer it to a large bowl and shred it with a hand mixer, then set aside.

2. **Make the Soup:** Add tortellini to the broth. Cook for 15 minutes over medium heat. Remove from heat and set aside.

3. In a large saucepan, melt butter over medium heat. Add flour, minced garlic, salt, and pepper. Continue cooking while whisking continuously. Once a paste forms, about 2 minutes, cook for another 3 minutes until bubbly. Then, while whisking slowly, add heavy cream and then 8 cups Homemade Chicken Stock and carrots. Continue cooking over medium heat for 15 minutes, stirring occasionally.

4. Add cream cheese and Italian cheese, stir, and reduce heat to low. Simmer for 15 minutes, stirring occasionally. Once cheeses are smooth and completely melted, add shredded chicken, spinach, and cooked tortellini. Stir, simmer for another 5 minutes, and serve.

Joshua's Famous Potato *and* Corn Chili *with* Corn Bread Biscuits

Joshua amazes me every single day; he is turning into such a good cook! Each January, our church has a chili cook-off for the men. When my boys were little, they would watch Dad make his chili or help him out. Now that they are older, they want to make their own special recipe for chili, hoping to beat Dad each year. I have to say, they are starting to figure out the spices to use in chili, and I think they may have matched Dad's chili—or possibly passed him up. Here is a recipe Joshua came up with that won second place!

Prep Time: 40 minutes
Cook Time: 1 hour and **20** minutes
Yields: 12 servings

Chili Ingredients:
2 pounds 90/10 lean ground beef
1 tablespoon minced fresh garlic
1 tablespoon ground white pepper
1 tablespoon garlic powder
1 tablespoon paprika
1 tablespoon dried minced onion
1 tablespoon garlic salt
2 tablespoons Worcestershire sauce
1 (28-ounce) can crushed tomatoes
2 (29-ounce) cans tomato sauce
2 (15-ounce) cans navy beans
1 (40-ounce) can chili beans
1 teaspoon crushed red pepper flakes
2 tablespoons chili powder
1 (32-ounce) bag frozen shredded hash browns
2 (14.5-ounce) cans fire-roasted corn

Corn Bread Ingredients:
2 (8.5-ounce) boxes corn muffin mix
2 large eggs
1 pound bacon, cooked crispy and crumbled (drippings reserved)
2/3 cup buttermilk
2 (4-ounce) cans chopped green chilies
1 (15.25-ounce) can southwest corn, drained

Steps:

1. **Make the Chili:** In a large saucepan, combine beef, minced garlic, white pepper, garlic powder, paprika, minced onion, garlic salt, and Worcestershire sauce. Cook over medium heat for 15 minutes, stirring occasionally. Stir in crushed tomatoes and reduce heat to low. Simmer for 5 minutes, stirring a few times. Set aside.

2. In a 10-quart stockpot, combine tomato sauce, navy and chili beans, red pepper flakes, and chili powder. Cook over low heat for 10 minutes.

3. Add meat mixture, hash browns, and fire-roasted corn to the stockpot. Stir and continue cooking for 25 minutes. While chili is cooking, start Corn Bread.

continued

continued

4. Preheat oven to 400°F.

5. **Make the Corn Bread:** Combine muffin mix, eggs, 2 tablespoons bacon grease, and buttermilk in a large bowl. Beat with a hand mixer for 2 minutes or until well combined.

6. Using a wooden spoon, fold in bacon, green chilies, and southwest corn.

7. Pour into a 12" round cast iron pan and bake for 25 minutes. Serve with Chili.

Green Chilie Taco Soup

This soup is so good, and it's perfect for those cold days when you need a little kick to warm your insides up. It's even better with a dollop of sour cream and some Cheddar cheese sprinkled on top, then garnished with a sprig of cilantro. It really does taste like a taco in a bowl. I make this often because it's so simple to make and tastes great. Plus, it easily freezes if you plan meals throughout the week.

Prep Time: 30 minutes
Cook Time: 45 minutes
Yields: 14 servings

Ingredients:

2 pounds 90/10 lean ground beef

2 pounds ground pork

1 large yellow onion, peeled and sliced thin

1 (10-ounce) bag matchstick carrots

2 (4-ounce) cans chopped green chilies

2 (10-ounce) cans fire-roasted tomatoes

2 tablespoons fresh lime juice

2 tablespoons minced fresh garlic

4 tablespoons ground cumin, divided

1 tablespoon garlic salt

2 tablespoons dried minced onion

1 tablespoon paprika

1 tablespoon ground white pepper

$\frac{1}{2}$ teaspoon cayenne pepper

2 (15-ounce) cans black beans

2 (15-ounce) cans navy beans

1 (29-ounce) can tomato sauce

8 cups beef broth

2 cups chopped fresh cilantro

4 cups shredded medium Cheddar cheese

2 cups sour cream

Steps:

1. In a 10-quart stockpot, combine beef, pork, onion, carrots, chilies, fire-roasted tomatoes, lime juice, minced garlic, and all dry seasonings except 2 tablespoons cumin. Cook over medium heat for 15 minutes, stirring occasionally. Do not drain juices.

2. To the same pot, add beans, tomato sauce, broth, and remaining 2 tablespoons cumin. Stir and cook for an additional 15 minutes over medium heat, then reduce heat to low and simmer for 15 more minutes.

3. Scoop into bowls and top each portion with cilantro, cheese, and sour cream. Serve.

Cheeseburger Soup

I remember the first time I made this: My family came in after work and school and could smell my cooking and asked what was for dinner, like they do every day. I told them it was Cheeseburger Soup. Every single one of my kids looked at me with a strange look on their face and scrunched up their nose. They immediately walked over to my huge stockpot and opened the lid. I seriously think they were expecting to see an actual cheeseburger sitting there!

Prep Time: 30 minutes
Cook Time: 1 hour
Yields: 12 servings

Ingredients:

4 pounds 90/10 lean ground beef

3 tablespoons minced fresh garlic

2 tablespoons dried minced onion

2 tablespoons garlic powder

2 tablespoons dried parsley

3 cups beef broth

3 cups whole milk

3 cups heavy cream

1 (8-ounce) block cream cheese

3 cups shredded medium Cheddar cheese

1 (2-pound) bag frozen shredded hash browns

1 tablespoon Himalayan salt

1 tablespoon ground black pepper

1 tablespoon onion powder

Steps:

1. In a large saucepan, combine beef, minced garlic, minced onion, garlic powder, and parsley. Cook over medium heat for 15 minutes, stirring occasionally.

2. Transfer meat mixture to a 10-quart stockpot over low heat and add broth. Simmer for 10 minutes, stirring occasionally.

3. Slowly add milk, heavy cream, cream cheese, and Cheddar. Continue cooking for 15 minutes, stirring often.

4. Add hash browns, salt, pepper, and onion powder. Cook for another 20 minutes. Make sure hash browns are thawed and cooked through. Serve.

Epilogue

WHAT A JOURNEY writing this cookbook has been. This process has helped me see what my language of love is: cooking for my loved ones. There are so many sweet memories that I had forgotten about but that through this journey came back to light. Writing this book has opened my eyes to more than just cooking, but how it was an integral part of our family growing and bonding. Sure, some may say it's just food, but for the Bell family it is the heart of our home. It started with little ones running all over the kitchen, sliding chairs across the floor to see what I was making, and sticking little fingers into the cookie dough, grabbing way more than they could eat at once. To now, my kids walking in the kitchen eager to see what's for dinner and telling me how work went or needing guidance on big decisions in their lives. These events all happened in our kitchen across from my cooktop. Sweet memories that will forever be engraved throughout our kitchen.

Now years later I'm seeing how our kitchen has been an important part of our family. It brings us together every single day through food but also as a gateway to conversation and to sharing our lives with each other. It's where we celebrate birthdays, holidays, and life's accomplishments. Hopefully, my kids will have so many great memories that they can talk about for years to come. Life is passing by so fast—I see my kids growing so much and becoming more independent—it is hard to just sit and watch. The best thing of all is, just when you think they don't need you anymore or want to hang out with you, they hug you and say I love you and thank you for all you've done for them. The sweetest part of that is they had no idea that we needed to hear that, but God did.

I am humbled by the opportunity God has given me to be able to share our family's adoption journey and the recipes we made throughout the years that were so important in bringing our family together, creating memories, and eventually leading to this wonderful cookbook to share with you. It's odd because I grew up having no interest in cooking and honestly not even caring about being in the kitchen. Nowadays, I am creating meals that are loved by not only my family but also thousands of others thanking me for sharing my simple, easy, and relatable meals for their families to enjoy. While writing this cookbook, so many people and memories came to mind as having helped in my journey not only as a cook but also as a wife and mother. They say it takes a village to raise a child, and I feel that it took a village to give me the courage to even begin this journey—and it took the constant encouragement from my sweet family to complete it. In a nutshell, I would have never, ever been able to accomplish this cookbook without the support of my family and friends.

Acknowledgments

IT'S AMAZING TO ME how when God has a plan for our lives, everything around us lines up just perfectly. He will bring those people into our lives that, at the time, we really don't know how much we need them or how they will play an important part in our lives. Well, I have many of those sweet humans that I would like to thank and dedicate this cookbook to.

First, my husband, Luke, who chose me to be his wife years ago knowing that according to the doctors I wouldn't be able to have children, but he still chose to spend the rest of his life with me. He was very patient during my early cooking phase and would try all my new recipes—and even though I could see the hesitation in his eyes, he gladly grabbed a plate and ate without complaining. My husband makes me want to be a better person, and he is the main reason I worked so hard in the kitchen making dinners that were fit for a king. He never asked me to do this, but it was my way of showing him through food how much I love him and am thankful for all he has done in my life.

Second, my eight sweet children, David, Robert, Joshua, Hailey, Brendon, Gideon, Izabella, and Noah. The number one question I get asked daily is how I have so much energy to accomplish all that I do, and it's because of them. They love me not only on my best days but also on my worst. I can remember the very first time each one of them called me Mom, and it was music

to my ears. Words can't describe how much I love my children, and they are the reason I get up each morning and head right to the kitchen to prepare something that I know they will love. What's awesome is, even if my meals are a flop, they will still eat them with smiles on their faces. (Well, some of them might scrunch up their nose, but they would at least try it!) Our family didn't come together in the normal way, but that's what makes us so unique; we all came together from different backgrounds and circumstances, but we love each other as if we have always been together. I'd describe us with one word: family.

Next, there are two women who are very important to me, and they are both the perfect example of being a godly wife and mother. They helped me start my cooking journey by bringing us fresh veggies from their garden and foods they had canned over the summer and fall to help me provide a nice meal for my then newly married husband. For years I watched these wonderful women own their kitchens and unselfishly serve the families they loved not only by presenting them with meals that could feed every child in the neighborhood but also by creating original dinner ideas that I had never seen before or eaten. They inspired me to become more comfortable in the kitchen and actually enjoy cooking for my family. What started out as a burden became something I could embrace and enjoy. In the kitchen, I found myself "borrowing" my husband's yellow work notebooks and writing down recipes plus new meal ideas. I wanted to create my own unique meals like these women did for their families. This made me so excited to head to the grocery store more to find the ingredients needed to make something extra special for our big family. Both of these amazing women not only made the best meals in town but also could bake like nobody's business. They both have a huge part in the woman, mother, and wife I am today. Thank you to my sweet mother, Sheila Storey, and my mother-in-law, Dodie Bell, for encouraging me and instilling in me the passion for cooking and baking.

Last, I am so grateful for my niece Destini Conard who spent hours searching out my recipes and writing things down to help me stay organized as we put the cookbook together. The best part is that this cookbook also helped us to grow closer as friends. Life gets busy as a mother, and the people you love can be put on a back burner at times, but this experience reconnected us with something we both are passionate about: cooking for our big families and growing as mothers.

But there is still one more person. Two months ago, I received an encouraging message from a sweet lady, sent at the exact moment that I needed it, and she started with this: "Have you ever thought about writing a cookbook?" She had no idea that I had been praying that God would help me find someone that could help turn my dreams of writing a cookbook into reality. This wouldn't have been possible without her believing in me, taking a chance herself to start this process of writing a cookbook, and her willingness to take the time to invest in me on this journey. Thank you, Danielle Kartes. I'm forever grateful.

To end, we all have a plan for our own lives, but life changes, and God brings wonderful people into our lives that we may not have realized we needed but that looking back we can see all the dots connected. It then just makes sense. Every one of us will be influenced by someone, and for me it was two women cooking with all their hearts for their families, then my husband standing by my side on my journey in becoming a mom and meeting each one of our children for the first time, and then two women who directly encouraged the creation of this cookbook so I could share my language of love. Thank you so much to all of you for your support of our family and story. I am forever grateful, thankful, and blessed.

Standard US/Metric Measurement Conversions

VOLUME CONVERSIONS

US Volume Measure	Metric Equivalent
1/8 teaspoon	0.5 milliliter
1/4 teaspoon	1 milliliter
1/2 teaspoon	2 milliliters
1 teaspoon	5 milliliters
1/2 tablespoon	7 milliliters
1 tablespoon (3 teaspoons)	15 milliliters
2 tablespoons (1 fluid ounce)	30 milliliters
1/4 cup (4 tablespoons)	60 milliliters
1/3 cup	90 milliliters
1/2 cup (4 fluid ounces)	125 milliliters
2/3 cup	160 milliliters
3/4 cup (6 fluid ounces)	180 milliliters
1 cup (16 tablespoons)	250 milliliters
1 pint (2 cups)	500 milliliters
1 quart (4 cups)	1 liter (about)

WEIGHT CONVERSIONS

US Weight Measure	Metric Equivalent
1/2 ounce	15 grams
1 ounce	30 grams
2 ounces	60 grams
3 ounces	85 grams
1/4 pound (4 ounces)	115 grams
1/2 pound (8 ounces)	225 grams
3/4 pound (12 ounces)	340 grams
1 pound (16 ounces)	454 grams

OVEN TEMPERATURE CONVERSIONS

Degrees Fahrenheit	Degrees Celsius
200 degrees F	95 degrees C
250 degrees F	120 degrees C
275 degrees F	135 degrees C
300 degrees F	150 degrees C
325 degrees F	160 degrees C
350 degrees F	180 degrees C
375 degrees F	190 degrees C
400 degrees F	205 degrees C
425 degrees F	220 degrees C
450 degrees F	230 degrees C

BAKING PAN SIZES

American	Metric
8 × 1 1/2 inch round baking pan	20 × 4 cm cake tin
9 × 1 1/2 inch round baking pan	23 × 3.5 cm cake tin
11 × 7 × 1 1/2 inch baking pan	28 × 18 × 4 cm baking tin
13 × 9 × 2 inch baking pan	30 × 20 × 5 cm baking tin
2 quart rectangular baking dish	30 × 20 × 3 cm baking tin
15 × 10 × 2 inch baking pan	30 × 25 × 2 cm baking tin (Swiss roll tin)
9 inch pie plate	22 × 4 or 23 × 4 cm pie plate
7 or 8 inch springform pan	18 or 20 cm loose bottom cake tin
9 × 5 × 3 inch loaf pan	23 × 13 × 7 cm or 2 lb narrow loaf or pâté tin
1 1/2 quart casserole	1.5 liter casserole
2 quart casserole	2 liter casserole

Index